GEORGES
BIZET'S *CARMEN*

Oxford KEYNOTES

Series Editor   KEVIN C. KARNES

GEORGES BIZET'S *CARMEN*

NELLY FURMAN

OXFORD
UNIVERSITY PRESS

Oxford University Press is a department of the University of Oxford. It furthers the University's objective of excellence in research, scholarship, and education by publishing worldwide. Oxford is a registered trade mark of Oxford University Press in the UK and certain other countries.

Published in the United States of America by Oxford University Press
198 Madison Avenue, New York, NY 10016, United States of America.

Library of Congress Cataloging-in-Publication Data
Names: Furman, Nelly, author.
Title: Georges Bizet's Carmen / Nelly Furman.
Description: New York : Oxford University Press, 2020. |
Includes bibliographical references and index.
Identifiers: LCCN 2019036000 (print) | LCCN 2019036001 (ebook) |
ISBN 9780190059149 (hardback) | ISBN 9780190059156 (paperback) |
ISBN 9780190059170 (epub) | ISBN 9780190059163 (updf) | ISBN 9780190059187 (online)
Subjects: LCSH: Bizet, Georges, 1838–1875. Carmen. | Meilhac, Henri, 1831–1897.
Carmen. | Mérimée, Prosper, 1803-1870. Carmen. | Romanies in opera.
Classification: LCC ML410.B62 F87 2020 (print) |
LCC ML410.B62 (ebook) | DDC 782.1—dc23
LC record available at https://lccn.loc.gov/2019036000
LC ebook record available at https://lccn.loc.gov/2019036001

9 8 7 6 5 4 3 2 1

Paperback printed by Marquis, Canada
Hardback printed by Bridgeport National Bindery, Inc., United States of America

CONTENTS

ACKNOWLEDGMENTS

DUE TO THE VAGARIES of life, family needs, and professional requirements, this book was in the making for many years. It owes a lot to a great number of people. To friends and students whose remarks sparked an idea, to the colleagues who, knowing my interest in *Carmen*, let me know that they had attended a performance, seen a film, or came across a mention of her name. I owe you all a most sincere debt of gratitude.

It all started in 1986, when Arthur Groos asked me to speak on *Carmen* at a conference on opera libretti that he and Roger Parker were organizing at Cornell University. My contribution to the conference's publication, *Reading Opera* (Princeton University Press, 1988), informs the chapter devoted here to *Carmen*'s libretto. Other colleagues from Cornell University: Cynthia Chase, Itsie (Isabel) Hull, Kathleen Long, Sally McConnell-Ginet, and Sandra Siegel, through their continued interest in my work, gave me the courage to persist. David Cope, David Goldberg, Judy Goulding, David Laurence, Dennis Looney, and Douglas Steward, with whom I worked at the Modern Language

Association, have also been relentless in their support. For the useful information they provided me, I also owe thanks to Sam Di Iorio, Evelyne Ender, and Sima Godfrey. Throughout my professional career, I benefited immensely from the support of Lawrence D. Kritzman of Dartmouth College and Domna Stanton of the Graduate Center of the City University of New York. To you all, I wish to express here my heartfelt appreciation for your friendship and help.

I was inspired by the writings of scholars from the United States and the United Kingdom who participated in the conference on *Carmen* in Newcastle on Tyne in 2002: Bruce Babington, Ann Davies, Chris Perriam, Phil Powrie, and Jeremy Tambling. They deserve special mention here. Susan McClary's work on *Carmen* served as a source for my own musings.

For her insights and generosity—as she had the misfortune of reading early versions of the manuscript—my deepest thanks go to Abby Zanger, who stoically and heroically faced the initial mess of my work, an amalgam of many years of research, and yet after reading and commenting on a daunting number of pages, she encouraged me to pursue.

John Ackerman extended his considerable knowledge and publishing experience in reviewing an early version. His suggestions helped me focus on key elements and organize my thoughts. I am most grateful for his help. I had the privilege over the years to appreciate his dedication to scholarship and enjoy his friendship.

I could not have asked for a more helpful reader than Kevin C. Karnes, the editor of the Keynotes series. His insightful remarks, attention to details, and intellectual generosity have informed every aspect of this book. I am deeply thankful. I also wish to thank Suzanne Ryan, executive music editor for Oxford University Press, who successfully shepherded this project to publication.

The friendship and generosity of time of Anne Shapiro who, from Ithaca and Los Angeles, keeps on listening to my woes and joys, were essential in helping me bring this project to a close. "Thank you" seems somehow too short an expression to acknowledge the importance of her help.

ABOUT THE COMPANION WEBSITE

OXFORD HAS CREATED A website to accompany *George Bizet's* Carmen. Material that cannot be made available in a book is provided here. The reader is encouraged to consult this resource while reading the book.

www.oup.com/us/gbc

INTRODUCTION

THE MAKING OF A MYTH

O NLY A FEW OF the countless tales told over the centuries are remembered generation after generation. It is difficult to say what makes a story at a given time more memorable than any other, but when a story's popularity persists, we confront a cultural event that invites further exploration. From the written page to the lyric stage and the silver screen, the story of Carmen is just such a cultural happening. When asked in 1983 why he chose to bring *Carmen*, as opposed to any other opera, to the stage in a completely reworked format, renowned director Peter Brook explained that very few operas were really popular. "Out of the ten most popular operas, there is one that is the most popular—*Carmen*. And it's not only an opera; it's a phenomenon."[1] Tchaikovsky, who hailed Bizet's *Carmen* as

Georges Bizet's Carmen. Nelly Furman, Oxford University Press (2020). © Oxford University Press.
DOI: 10.1093/oso/9780190059149.001.0001

a masterpiece, accurately predicted the opera's astonishing success: "I am convinced," he wrote, "that within some ten years or so *Carmen* will be the most popular opera in the world."[2] Today, the name of Carmen and the sounds of Bizet's music are recognized across continents. Carmen qualifies as an iconic figure, and Bizet's instantly recognized score proclaims her eminence as a referential sign on the world's cultural stages.

One of the most beguiling figures born of the nineteenth-century imagination, Carmen made her first public appearance in a novella by Prosper Mérimée, published in 1845. Thirty years later, Georges Bizet immortalized her on the lyric stage. Since that time, she has been the heroine of several ballets[3] and over seventy feature films, many produced by illustrious international directors, from Charlie Chaplin to Otto Preminger, Carlos Saura, Jean-Luc Godard, and Ramaka Geï. She has appeared in Broadway musicals and even attracted the world's attention at the 1988 Winter Olympics, when both of the two top women figure skaters chose Bizet's score for their individual programs, an encounter dubbed "the Battle of the Carmens."[4]

In moving from print to the lyric stage and from opera to the silver screen, the story of Carmen has been endlessly rewritten—authored by many, and thus (as it were) fathered by none. In fact, the story's earliest published version, Mérimée's 1845 novella, is actually not its first account, for in one of his letters Mérimée tells us that he heard it from a woman friend.[5] Past and present renderings of Carmen give different inflections to the story, which, in each of its remakes, mirrors the changing concerns and shifting values of individual authors and their societies. It is precisely through this process of repetition and change across countries, generations, and media that Carmen has attained the status of myth.

Because the mythic process is one of constant repetition and change, the first recorded history of a myth does not necessarily explain its subsequent versions, nor is the most recent version a cumulative product or totalizing rendering of the story as such. There is, says the anthropologist Claude Lévi-Strauss, "no single 'true' version of which all the others are but copies or distortions. Every version belongs to the myth."[6] Accordingly, one can apprehend any occurrence of the story as a starting point for analysis. While Mérimée's novella is the founding literary text, the version that actually set the story on its mythical course is not the novella but Bizet's opera, which can be credited with launching a cultural industry bearing the unofficial trademark of Carmen's name. Although Mérimée's novella precedes the opera by thirty years, it is the popularity of the opera and the filmic renditions of the story that inflect our understanding of Mérimée's narrative. Hence my decision to anchor this study in the opera's libretto, and break the linearity of time by a turn back to the novella followed by a jump forward to the cinematic medium, discussing some memorable films in which Carmen is portrayed before considering the deployment of themes and other elements that may account for the story's success.

There is, of course, no single path to understanding myths; like other cultural artifacts, myths belong at one and the same time to several modes of expression and representation. Thus they can be analyzed punctually, synchronically, or diachronically, and, like other cultural artifacts, they can be shown to respond in different ways to different methods of interpretation. Whether the plot of a mythic story is relegated to the past or projected into the future, whenever it is retold, re-presented, or evoked, it speaks to our present concerns, and it addresses us in contemporary terms. Reappropriated by passing generations for any number of purposes, myths reflect the perceived needs, anxieties, and unacknowledged issues of a society. Often we think of myths as originating in preliterate societies, or at least we consider them as legends born in ancient times. Even those inscribed in writing—a relatively new medium when set against oral traditions—were often inscribed initially at some temporal distance from our present: the Oedipus myth belongs to ancient Greece; the story of Romeo and Juliet was popularized by Shakespeare; Spain's Golden Age left us Don Quixote, created by Cervantes, and Don Juan, attributed to the dramatist Tirso de Molina. These myths, to list but a few, would inspire some of the most famous composers in the Western tradition: Mozart's *Don Giovanni*, Gounod's *Romeo and Juliet*, and Stravinsky's *Oedipus Rex*. But while these and many other operas have been inspired by myths that originated in earlier times, *Carmen* is perhaps the only opera that spawned its own mythic future. For Carmen is a modern myth, a myth born out of the French imagination in the first half of the nineteenth century.

France in the nineteenth century was a new bourgeois nation, a country engaged in colonial expansion and caught in the dynamics of the industrial revolution, which, along with its benefits, brought contingent social unrest. Besides these socioeconomic realities, the country was also caught in the throes of swiftly changing cultural paradigms. Chiefly, perhaps, the ideals of an earlier romanticism were slowly being replaced by the so-called objective views of positivism, supported by an unflinching faith in progress. Science, of course, held the promise of a better future, and its accomplishments were spectacular: from steamboats and the mechanical printing press to medical discoveries that stopped the spread of disease-causing microorganisms. Established fields of knowledge exploded into new areas of study with the establishment of the social sciences, which were expected to produce solutions to existing social woes. Both Mérimée's novella and Bizet's opera reflect these aspects of life in nineteenth-century France. However, as its extraordinary popularity and numerous international adaptations of the twentieth and twenty-first centuries imply, the story of Carmen continues to be relevant to many today. Musicologist Susan McClary puts it bluntly: "if we were not still stuck in the dilemmas Mérimée and Bizet point to, we would not be witnessing the endless stream of *Carmen* productions on stage, film, and TV."[7]

The goal of this study is to attempt to understand the lasting pertinence of *Carmen*: to account for the success of the story in the industrial age, to discern its attraction in our own cinematic era, to describe the elements of the story that give it its cultural salience and resonance, and to understand these features as markers of both the social realities and the cultural unconscious of our times. What accounts for the popularity of the story of Carmen beyond the lyric stage? Why has this story become a cultural phenomenon? What elements of the plot attract artists across media? These are some of the questions that beckon attention.

In *The Magic Mountain*, Thomas Mann has Hans Castorp, the novel's protagonist, summarize the plot of Bizet's opera, in order to show that the young man has successfully overcome his feelings for an attractive seductress:

> I once read a story—no, I saw it in the theater—about how a good-hearted young fellow . . . gets involved with an enchanting Gypsy—and she was enchanting, with a flower behind her ear, a savage, mischievous creature, and he was so fascinated with her that he got completely off-track, sacrificed everything for her, deserted the colors, ran off with her to join a band of smugglers and disgraced himself in every way. And after he had done all that, she had enough of him, and came along with a matador, a compelling personality with a splendid baritone. It ended outside the bullring, with the little soldier, his face chalky white, his shirt unbuttoned, stabbing her with a knife, though you might say she as good as planned the whole thing herself.[8]

If we are to accept Mann's summary, it would appear that the opera is about a soldier named Don José.

But the same plot looks different if told from Carmen's perspective, which one might summarize as follows:

> To thank him for letting her escape, Carmen, a Gypsy, bestows her favors on José, a corporal in the dragoons. He falls in love with her, abandons the army, and joins the Gypsies. But Carmen soon tires of his constant jealousy, and when he leaves to visit his dying mother, she gets involved with a matador. José returns and kills her.

Like any retelling, summarizing a plot is an interpretive act, a forceful muting of some voices of the text, an option selected from among various reading strategies, evidence of an ideological stance. *Carmen*, of course, is not exclusively *his* story, any more than it is *her* story; nor is it simply *their* story, for it is at the same time *my* story of his, her, and their stories (Figure I.1).

For some opera lovers, *Carmen* tells the story of a soldier who falls in love with an enticing and unfaithful Gypsy whom he kills. For them, *Carmen* is first of all the tragic story of a man's passionate love for a woman who spurns him. For others, however, it is rather the tragic story of a woman's fight for the freedom to love as she pleases. Yet the pathos of the story resides perhaps neither in *his* story nor in *her* story but in *their* story—that is to say, in the fact that José's and Carmen's desires exclude each other. Unlike so many other operatic plots, Bizet's opera contains no external circumstances for the lovers to overcome: no

FIGURE I.1   Image from a staging of *Carmen* at the London Royal Ballet choregraphed by Carlos Acosta, set designed by Tim Hatley, October 27, 2015.

objections by family members, no interdiction proffered by king or emperor, no stated religious, moral, or political precepts that would preclude their coming together. José's passion and jealousy deny Carmen her need for freedom; he cannot live without her, she cannot live with him. Their antithetical desires render the two lovers fundamentally incompatible. In this respect, the opera stages not simply a tragic love story but rather the tragedy of love itself, where love is conceived as the romantic and romanticized union of individuals who complement each other with equal reciprocity in their feelings, and also have similar needs, identical taste, and a shared vision. In *Carmen,* love is presented as the locus of an impossible coming together, which is why there can be no love duet between the protagonists.

For audiences in this post-romantic age, the unattainable dream of the perfect union may resonate with particular force. Carmen and José stand at the extremes on the spectrum of that thing—that feeling, drive, or instinct—called *love.* Arrayed between them, spectators identify with one or the other protagonist in relation to their personal needs and understandings of the dynamics at work in any intimate relationship. Thus, in the age of women's liberation, Carmen's yearning for freedom may elicit solidarity, while José's loss of self may inspire dread. For the individual as for a community, these are universal and enduring topics.

Literary texts have provided the plots for many operas, and many French works of the nineteenth century have inspired composers. Victor Hugo's plays served as the basis for Verdi's *Hernani* and *Rigoletto,* and for *La Traviata* Verdi turned to *La Dame aux camélias* by Alexandre Dumas (fils). But Mérimée's *Carmen* is an unusual kind of novella for operatic adaptation, for it purports to recount the adventures of a French traveler doing historical research in Spain. It thus presents itself at the juncture of literature and science, as both a work of narrative fiction and an ethnological study of the people of Roma. The love story of Carmen and José, as recounted to the French traveler by José himself, is relegated to the third chapter of Mérimée's book. And although it offers a heartbreaking love story in an exotic landscape—two elemental ingredients of romantic narrative—Mérimée's *Carmen* nonetheless seems an odd choice as the source of inspiration for an opera.

The Roma have been objects of fascination for Western artists and explorers throughout the ages. However, as a character molded by nineteenth-century ideology, the figure of Carmen belongs to a specific time and place. For the social scientists of the nineteenth century, the Roma, a nomadic society linked by a distinct oral language, presented a particularly enticing subject of analysis. Their origins were obscure, their language little known, and their nomadic lifestyle unfathomable. Yet, despite attempts to coerce them into normative European societies, they had succeeded in preserving their traditional ways. Whereas historians and ethnologists attempted to establish their origins by studying their trades and social mores, linguists argued that they were of Indian descent by demonstrating that their language, Romany, was etymologically rooted in Indic. In the nineteenth century, researchers in the nascent sciences of ethnology and linguistics sought to prove or disprove the biblical claim that all mankind had descended through Noah and his sons from Adam.[9] The prevalent hypothesis in this search for the ancestry of

Western societies was to be found in the suggestion that Europe was populated by descendants of tribes that had migrated west from India. By linking Romany to Indic, linguists claimed to have provided proof that the Roma or Gypsies, as they were called, were precisely such a tribe. In this respect, the story told in Mérimée's novella could be said to fulfill one of the traditional functions of myth, that of answering questions of origin and explaining the mysteries of ancestry. Called "Tinkers" or "Travelers" in the United Kingdom, "Zigeuner" in Germany, and "Gitanos" in Spain, in France the Roma have been called "Tziganes," "Gitans," "Bohémiens," "Romanichels," or "Calès." The Roma consider the name "Gypsy" a pejorative term. "Gypsy" is a cognate of the name Egypt because the Roma were mistakenly thought to have come from Egypt. In Mérimée's novella, Carmen refers to her activities as "les affaires d'Egypte." Regrettably the term Gypsy will often appear in this study because it is the word used in the translations from the French and it is the identifier associated with Carmen.

In the novella, the Roma are fearsome bandits; in the opera's they are playful, lighthearted smugglers only fearful of being caught. Introduced primarily for exotic purposes, the ethnic element allows Bizet to include presumed Spanish rhythms in his score. Central to Bizet's opera is the love story between protagonists, linked, as it were, as victim and victimizer. But in Mérimée's narrative the theme of freedom and dependency is attached to the encounter between the narrator and the strangers he meets, strangers at once curiously attractive and deeply feared. In the novella, the traveler's first encounter with

José, the outlaw, leads the narrator to ask what the moral obligation and limits of responsibility are to self and others in a given situation. Though less salient in the opera, this is perhaps the theme that speaks most forcefully to contemporary concerns. It certainly may help to account for the making of the Carmen myth. As Roger Callois suggests, "it is in myth that one best seizes in its immediacy the link between the most secret and virulent postulations of the individual psyche and the most imperative and troubling pressures of social existence."[10] And, as Julia Kristeva points out, encounters with a foreigner can lead to divergent reactions, which make plain just such troubling pressures: "'I am at least as remarkable, and therefore I love him,' the observer thinks; 'now I prefer my own peculiarity, and therefore I kill him.'"[11] To love the other in his or her sameness, or to kill that other because he or she appears most of all different, are psychic reactions to another person. Love and hate are two sides of the same emotional affect. Adam Phillips summarizes the opposing feelings of love and hate in the following way:

> Love and hate—a too simple vocabulary, and so never quite the right names—are the common source, the elemental feelings with which we apprehend the world; they are interdependent in the sense that you can't have one without the other, and that they mutually inform each other. The way we hate people depends on the way we love them and vice versa. According to psychoanalysis these contradictory feelings enter into everything we do. We are ambivalent, in Freud's view, about anything and everything that matters to us; indeed, ambivalence is the way we recognise that someone or something has become significant to us.[12]

The tragic story of José and Carmen in Bizet's opera and the traveler's adventures in Mérimée's narrative are only unrecognized or unrecognizable as similar because they are presented as a traditional romantic relationship on stage and in the form of both a lovers' story and also an homosocial interaction between the traveler and the bandit.

Mérimée's text, Bizet's opera, and cinematic renditions of the story of Carmen, in their concealed or overt misogyny and/or racism (or, inversely, in their overt or concealed feminism and/or universal solidarity), all speak to some of the anguishing social torments of our time: loss of self and identity, our attraction to and repulsion from otherness, our competing needs for dependency and freedom. Modern discourses reflect these national, collective, and personal crises in the frequent usage of such words as multiculturalism, sex, gender, class, and ethnicity. Racism, misogyny, and loss of self can be apprehended as psychic mechanisms of reaction to fears of sameness occluded by the sight of difference. Conversely, certain forms of self-affirmation or glorification of otherness may be denials of difference. Modern cinematic versions of *Carmen*, from Otto Preminger's all-black cast in *Carmen Jones* (1954) to the flock of international Carmens in 1983—Rosi's obsessive bullfighting metaphor, Saura's exacerbated nationalism, Godard's parody—and the new millennium's African productions (Ramaka's vibrant Senegalese woman, the celebratory South African *U-Carmen*), each in its own way confronts issues of identity, otherness, and social conflicts. One can predict that as political and social contexts change, so too will the Carmens who greet new generations of readers, listeners, and spectators.

Myths are stories people tell and retell to explain things to themselves and others. The pages that follow, which explore the significance of the Carmen stories, constitute in themselves yet another version of the Carmen myth, a fable told by this interpreter. "It does not appear," says Roger Callois, "that the ability to create or experience myths has been supplanted by that of commenting on them."[13] In the end, it is reassuring to know that texts, independently of our efforts to interpret them, continue to speak for themselves.

CHAPTER 1

FATAL ATTRACTION

AFTER BECOMING DISENCHANTED WITH his musical idol Richard Wagner, Nietzsche found in Bizet's *Carmen* the "art of the future," the antithesis to Wagner's decadent modernism. For Nietzsche, both Bizet's music and the realism of the story were worthy of enthusiastic praise. In his view, Wagner's exemplar of tender devotion, Senta, the heroine of *The Flying Dutchman*, evoked an idealized vision of love, whereas Bizet's concept of love as a deadly struggle for possession reflected the reality of gender relations:

> Finally, love, love that has been translated back into *nature*! *Not* the love of a "higher virgin"! No Senta-sentimentality! But instead, love as fate, as *fatality*, cynical, innocent, cruel—and that is precisely what makes it *nature*! Love, whose method is war, whose basis is the *deadly hatred* between the sexes!—I do not

Georges Bizet's Carmen. Nelly Furman, Oxford University Press (2020). © Oxford University Press.
DOI: 10.1093/oso/9780190059149.001.0001

know any other place where the tragic wit that is the essence of love expresses itself so strongly, is formulated with so much horror as in Don José's last cry, which brings the work to an end:

Yes! *I* have killed her,
I—my beloved Carmen![1]

The sentimental relationship represented in Wagner's *Flying Dutchman* was, according to Nietzsche, essentially a product of culture, while the passionate feelings expressed by Carmen and José were truer to nature. Leaving aside the question of love's connection to a concept of nature as opposed to culture, for Nietzsche what clearly changed between Wagner's Senta and Carmen is the vision, the essence of love, its very nature. The ideals of complementarity and mutual dependency of the sexes played out in Wagner had been replaced in Bizet's opera by a failure of reciprocity: by a basic incompatibility between lovers. In Bizet's work, love is not founded on a notion of preconceived oneness, but rather presents a problem of irreconcilable differences. The originality of *Carmen* is due precisely to the fact that its lovers are *not* made for each other. They have opposing needs and an equal say in voicing their antithetical desires. Hence the work's dramatic tension: instead of seeing two lovers yearning to be together, we watch them struggling to satisfy their individual needs and desires.

Traditional interpretations of Bizet's *Carmen* imply that the soldier's downfall was caused by his devotion to an attractive but unworthy woman. They propose a view of José as a victim: victim of his own naïveté, of his upbringing, of his obsessional passion; or, conversely, he is seen as a victim

FIGURE 1.1   Clip from the Salzburg Festival, 2012. Magdelana Kozena and
Jonas Kaufmann.

of Carmen's beguiling beauty, enticing manner, or supposedly demonic nature. In this conventional argument, José
is the dupe of a woman who uses her attraction to reduce
her lover to a debased and impoverished condition. She is a
female vampire and he is her prey. For Mario Praz, Carmen
must be counted among a long list of *femmes fatales* because her "diabolical feminine fascination" brings about "a

violence of passion that makes the man lose all regard for his own social position."[2] For Michel Leiris, there was no doubt that Carmen's death is just retribution:

> Carmencita—who stabs one of her companions in the cigar factory and ridicules the wretch [José] whom she has forced to desert until he kills her; mistress of a matador who dedicates the beast he is about to kill to her, as to a bloodthirsty goddess for whom he must risk death—the lovely Carmencita, before being murdered, is indeed a murderess.[3]

The corollary of this psychological argument is that when José stabs Carmen, his murder is seen as an act of self-defense, the means by which he regains his manhood. In a 2007 cultural history of films devoted to Carmen, one reads: "By killing Carmen, the outlaw José becomes *don* José once more, ennobled through sacrifice."[4] But in an opera guide of 1982, José is no longer Carmen's victim; rather, he has been transformed into a "real" man by Carmen and he only loses his manhood when he abandons Carmen in order to return to his mother's deathbed:

> Rather than the weak soldier who renounces his duties to follow a dangerous seducer (which is how he too often appears), Bizet's Don José is a man whose fatal vocation compels him to abandon a pale sentimental love and banal occupations, and to plunge into what he does not know—the outlaw world of passion. . . . Don José begins to live when he meets Carmen: love acts as a second birth, transforming a rather ectoplasmic character into a full-blooded man. One could argue that if he shows any weakness it is not by following Carmen, but by being unable to follow her completely. He returns to his dying mother

instead of responding to Carmen's vital challenge; he is not a free man and he loses her.[5]

In this analysis, José seems a prime candidate for men's liberation. Here, it is José's mother, rather than Carmen, who has an adverse hold on the soldier. Whether it is José's attachment to Carmen or his mother that spells his doom, the function of the woman remains the same—that of man's torturer.

If, however, we read the opera not as the story of José, but as the story of Carmen's struggle for freedom, then the roles of victim and torturer become reversed. It is no longer José but Carmen who suffers. A case could be made that, psychologically, Carmen is as much the victim of José's possessiveness and jealousy as he feels himself to be the victim of her charms. When, in the last act, she confronts him and forces the issue, her gesture of self-affirmation acquires the dimension of a political act. In *Opera, or the Undoing of Women*, Catherine Clément calls Carmen "the most feminist, the most stubborn of these dead women," the one who embodies "the dark and revolutionary proclamation of a woman who chooses to die before a man decides it for her."[6] One could, however, respond to Clément's assertion by arguing that when Carmen chooses to risk her life by standing up to her lover, her suicidal gesture might also be interpreted as a victory for José, his social values, and his understanding of love as dependence. Yet despite the conflicting interpretations that Carmen's death may elicit, her struggle for personal freedom has assured her a place in the pantheon of feminist idols.

The antithetical interpretations elicited by Bizet's opera are not limited to feminist politics. In a 1925 production of *Carmen* in Moscow, José is seduced by a Jewish girl to the communist cause.[7] In Frank Corsaro's 1984 staging of the work for the New York City Opera, set during the Spanish Civil War, Carmen is portrayed as a freedom fighter who falls in the struggle against fascism. On the other hand, in a fascist staging of the opera at Pforzheim during the Third Reich, Carmen personified the danger awaiting innocent youth, who could, by fraternizing with the local population, easily be bewitched by a member of an ethnic group designated as inferior by the Nazis.[8]

As these examples make clear, Bizet's opera has been produced to advance distinctive political ideologies that may even be patently opposed to one another. It has been hailed as representative of the feminist struggle and at the same time denounced as a vehicle for sexist propaganda, staged as a pro-communist manifesto, perceived as an anti-fascist play, and presented to illustrate Nazi racist dictums. While many cultural artifacts are open to differing viewpoints, few have been as systematically enlisted in the making of contradictory claims. Theodor Adorno remarked that Bizet's work resides at the exact midpoint between opposites, at the moment of absolute incompatibility between potential readings, hence the impossibility of assigning to it a fixed, overarching meaning. *Carmen* defies any "totality of meaning" that would allow for the possibility of transcending oppositions; rather, the opera succeeds in maintaining a "prohibition on transcendence."[9]

Whether we see José as victim or Carmen as martyr, we are forever caught in a reversible structure, the mirroring image of a master/slave relationship where the two protagonists are dependent on each other, even inverted reflections of each other. In the corrida of passionate love, Carmen and José both occupy in turn the position of matador and bull. The text of the opera itself suggests the interchangeability of the two roles: structurally, by having Carmen wield a knife in the first act and having José stab her in the last; linguistically, by having Escamillo name a bull after Carmen; grammatically, by making it impossible to determine whether the eye referred to in Escamillo's signature aria belongs to the woman or the bull ("Remember, while you are fighting, that a dark eye watches you, and that love awaits you").[10] On stage, the interchangeability of their positions is indicated visually by having Carmen wear a red dress, reminiscent of the matador's cape and the colors in his costume, as well as by having her hide part of her face with her mantilla while José dons dark pants and a white shirt—the very colors of a bull's markings. Bull or matador, matador or bull? As Dominique Maingueneau notes in his own study of *Carmen*, one of the great strengths of Bizet's opera is the way in which it makes opting for one or another of these interpretations impossible.[11]

GENDER QUESTIONS: ROLES AND VOICES

Because of its oppositional structures, Bizet's opera would seem particularly well suited to illustrate a war between the sexes. Yet interestingly enough, in the area of sexual difference, the polarities are not *between* the sexes but *within* each gender. That is to say, between characters who embody traditional middle-class standards of femininity and masculinity, and protagonists who appear, in relation to those standards, as less-than-perfect representatives of their sex: Micaëla in contrast to Carmen, the virgin and the whore; or Escamillo compared to José, virility versus effeminacy. Significantly, the figures of Micaëla and Escamillo do not appear in Mérimée's story. Invented by the librettists Henri Meilhac and Ludovic Halévy, they are stock characters in the *opéra comique* tradition. Micaëla represents the model of chaste femininity, Escamillo appears as the paragon of masculinity. In terms of gender, they serve as foils to the main characters. In Act III, which takes place in what Micaëla calls *un lieu sauvage*, a natural (or non-civilized) mountainous spot, she and Escamillo do not interact. She comes in after he has left. Absence of interaction, not war, characterizes the relationship between these traditional exemplars of the two sexes. With respect to relations between the sexes, Bizet's *Carmen* does not support Nietzsche's assertion as to their "deadly hatred," but rather appears to illustrate Barthes's contention that "Sex is a tragic privilege in so far as it is the first element of the original conflict: it is not the sexes that create the conflict, but the conflict that defines the sexes."[12]

Bizet's musical score suggests similar gender polarities. In accordance with the nineteenth-century operatic code that orders the distribution of voices and interactions of roles, Carmen's lower-range mezzo (the role of Carmen can also be sung by a contralto) could no more blend with José's lyrical tenor than Micaëla's lyrical soprano could be united with Escamillo's baritone. In *Idéologies de l'opéra*, Philippe-Joseph Salazar delineates the typology of operatic roles as a homologous relational system between the family unit and the singers' vocal range.[13] To the family trinity *Father-Daughter-Lover* (bass or baritone, soprano, and tenor), there corresponds by necessity the role of *Mother/Rival*, with its lower-range voice. In Bizet's opera, Micaëla occupies the position of the Daughter, while Carmen is typologically at once the Lover and the formal Mother/Rival, hence the range of tessituras possible for her role.

For Salazar, the nineteenth-century enthronement of the mezzo, who can blend together the highest tones of the male castrato and the deepest dramatic effects of the female contralto, presents a particular ideal of beauty, a beauty that is trans- or intersexual, as transgressive in the anatomic physicality of the castrato as in the musical range of the mezzo.[14] Clément points out that in nineteenth-century opera, "the ones sacrificed were always sopranos and tenors, whether they were men or women," and this is because they were in "the tessitura of youth and innocence."[15] No wonder, then, that public sympathy is so often directed not to Carmen but to José, the lyrical tenor. In the lyrical code of nineteenth-century opera, once described as the coming together of a soprano and a tenor over the objections of a baritone, the acceptable, that is to say sanctified, love duet would consist in the blending of the voices of Micaëla and José. Hence, in the first act, when José and Micaëla harmoniously unite their voices in the aria "Ma mère je la vois!," the duet serves as a referential backdrop, a reminder that *this* is the form of love that has a legitimate place on the operatic stage (Example 2.1). In this duet, Micaëla has no story of her own to tell; she acts as the perfect "Echo" to José's "Narcissus," simply repeating his words. "My mother, I see her! Yes, my village stands before my eyes," sings José, and Micaëla reaffirms his evocation in the third person: "He remembers his mother."

Unlike Micaëla and Escamillo, Carmen and José are far from embodying traditional gender ideals for their sexes. From the beginning of the opera, we face a world divided according to sex. Across from the cigar factory—which no man is permitted to enter—stands the guardhouse, a male enclave that Micaëla refuses to enter. Only in the public square between these two buildings are men and women free to mingle.[16] When compelled by his superiors to enter the prohibited female area of the factory, José pays with his virility. On stage, soldiers form a barrier around Carmen, effectively separating her from the other women. One could argue that by wielding a knife and her courage in the face of death, Carmen exhibits supposedly manly characteristics, whereas José's dependence on a woman, as well as the simple fact that he is in love, makes him seem a lesser man. As Hélène Cixous has remarked, "being possessed is not desirable for a masculine imaginary, which would interpret it as passivity—a dangerous feminine position."[17] And Barthes notes that "a man is not feminized because he is inverted, but because he is in love."[18]

Through Micaëla and Escamillo, the librettists Meilhac and Halévy affirm conventional notions of sexual difference, while simultaneously blurring gender differentiation in the characters of Carmen and José. No longer characters endowed with stock-gendered personae, Carmen and José suggest rather the possibility of mixed gender features within each sex. One could thus argue, contra Nietzsche, that Bizet's opera does not represent a war between the sexes; rather, it skillfully illustrates the polarities within each gender, and the congruence of identity between the two. This ambivalence in gender roles may help explain the enduring popularity of the opera among both men and women, who might identify with the protagonists according to a conventional male/female divide, or recognize themselves psychologically in either of the protagonists across gender lines.

THE CRUELTY AND GENEROSITY OF LOVE

For Nietzsche, the war of the sexes is only an expedient for depicting love in its violent cruelty. Indeed, the greatness of Bizet's opera—and Nietzsche insists upon this—is due to the violence of its vision of love:

> This sort of perspective on love (the only one worthy of a philosopher—) is a rarity: it raises a work of art above thousands of others. Because, on average, artists are like everyone else, only worse—they *misunderstand* love. . . . Everyone thinks that people in love are selfless because they want to advance the interests of another person, often at their own expense. But in return, they want to *possess* that other person. . . . Even God is no exception here. . . . he becomes terrible if you do not love him in return.[19]

Placed here among the figures of the philosopher, the superior artist, and God, José finds himself in distinguished company. In the opera, however, José is the only one who feels that his love is a proprietary right. Escamillo, for example, patiently awaits his turn. Even Micaëla has no desire to hold on to José, for in Act III she refers to him as "the one I *once* loved" (*Celui que j'aimais jadis*). Nor is José *always* possessive: as soon as Carmen enters the picture, he easily lets go of Micaëla, his mother's love choice for him.

Rather, possessiveness is the characteristic feature of José's love for Carmen alone. Unlike José, Carmen equates love with freedom, as that which can be enjoyed but not owned, celebrated but not imposed. "Love is the child of bohemia," she sings in Act I; "it knows no law. . . . You think you hold it, it avoids you. You think you are avoiding it, it has taken hold of you."[20] Commenting upon Nietzsche's statement, Adorno remarked of Carmen: "Her generosity of soul is not to lay claim to any and therefore not to desire to possess or keep anything."[21] With José, the opera paints love as a painful and overpowering feeling, whereas with Carmen, it depicts love as an emotion that neither hinges on suffering nor determines self-annihilation. Through Carmen and José, Bizet's opera presents the perennial conflict between passion as a fixed and all-consuming bondage and love as an unfettered bonding.[22]

Incapable of choosing an object of love for and by himself, José acts and reacts in terms of others: his mother, his lieutenant, or the matador. It was at his mother's suggestion that he once looked on Micaëla as a love object: "Do not fear, mother, your son will obey. He will do what you tell him. I love Micaëla, I'll make her my wife," he sings in Act I.[23] Whereas all the soldiers court Carmen, José at first shows no interest in her. It is she who, intrigued by his indifference, forces him to notice her. If it were not for the unexpected return of Lieutenant Zuniga at the end of Act II, José would have left Carmen and returned to his barracks. In the last act, José's words to her are revealing, for it is not love but his regret at having forgone his chance at salvation—and his fear that she will laugh at him in the arms of his rival—that prompts him to kill her: "So, I have lost my very soul so that you can run away, you harlot, and laugh at me from his arms!"[24] For José, desire is always triggered by someone else, determined by another. As René Girard defined it, in such a triangle of desire "it is the rival who should be accorded the dominant role," for "the subject desires the object because the rival desires it."[25] Carmen, whose charms are not powerful enough to keep José when the bugle sounds in Act II, becomes irresistible to José when another man covets her. The chaste Micaëla can be abandoned because a widowed mother, no matter how phallic and fetishized she may be, is no match for the real rival—the absent father—or for another man's gaze.[26] Barthes summarizes it this way: "Jealousy is an equation made of three interchangeable (undecidable) terms. One is always simultaneously jealous of two people: I am jealous of whom I love and of who loves my lover."[27]

For Girard, such mimetic desire is the operating principle in all human relationships, and this of necessity leads to violence, a violence averted through the ritual sacrifice of some scapegoat. In the Girardian model, Carmen occupies the position of the bull, a sacrificial animal immolated for the common good on the altar of violence. Another way of conceiving this triadic system is to focus on the function assumed by Carmen as mediator between parties. As the common object of desire by both the lieutenant and José, or by the matador and José, Carmen stands as the connector of José to other men. Or, to quote Luce Irigaray, in such a system, "woman exists only as the possibility of mediation, transaction, transition, transference between man and his fellow-creatures, indeed, between man and himself."[28] As the connecting link between two men, Carmen is in fact neither the matador nor the bull—she is more like the matador's cape, the lure with which the matador goads his opponent and behind which he hides his sword until the moment of truth.[29] Once lifted, the cape reveals the likeness of the two combatants, unveiling subjects who, like Narcissus, are trapped in their own gaze. In José's passionate love, Carmen becomes a projection of himself. In this triangle of mimetic desire, the triad becomes a dyad, and the dyad becomes a one.

José is possessive, not because he is possessed by some other, but because the other is himself. In José's case, love is a narcissistic eroticism, the bond of a man caught in the gaze of his own reflection, for whom the other is only an extension of the self. In this perspective, Carmen is indeed a *femme fatale*, as Mary Ann Doane defines her:

> The femme fatale is an articulation of fears surrounding the loss of stability and centrality of the self, the "I," the ego. These anxieties appear quite explicitly in the process of her representation as castration anxiety. The power accorded to the femme fatale is a function of fears linked to the notions of uncontrollable drives, the fading of subjectivity, and the loss of conscious agency—all themes of the emergent theories of psychoanalysis. But the femme fatale is situated as evil and is frequently punished or killed.[30]

From Carmen's perspective, however, it is not the lover but the freedom to love that matters, to love without constraints. The lover is not, for her, an extension of *herself*. Her object of desire is desire itself—and not simply to be desired, but to be herself desiring. In the famous Habanera of Act I, an aria that stands as her *ars erotica*, she describes love as unpredictable, uncontrollable, and absent when you want it, yet present when you no longer await it. It appears when and where you least expect it.

Carmen's Habanera is composed of free-floating stanzas of varying lengths, with three different voices skillfully interlaced. First, there are descriptive passages in the impersonal, collective third person. After the impersonal third person, Carmen switches to the first person. Finally, the second person comes into the song with the line, "If you don't love me" (*Si tu ne m'aimes pas*). When she sings this line, Carmen is almost always seen addressing some young man. But although she says "you," her words are part of a monologue; this feigned dialogue is but a rhetorical figure, an apostrophe; the "you" she addresses is also herself (Example 2.2).

Carmen's vision of love does not exclude narcissism, but it proposes in addition to this specular "I"/"you" relationship an impersonal third-person pronoun, at once singular and plural: the "one" to which she refers in the first stanza, when she sings, "It is in vain that one summons it" (*C'est bien en vain qu'on l'appelle*). While Carmen's "I" and "you" are reflections of each other, the pronoun "one" designates the possibility of someone else, marks the space of the other. This pronoun opens a space for a third instance that undermines a subject-object relationship and its mimetic closure, a third instance that plays a mediating role between the self as subject and the self objectivized in "you" under the guise of otherness, as we find in the case of José's narcissistic understanding of love. In their final encounter, when José implores her to return to him, she does not use the first person but addresses him in the second person and couches her voice in the third person: "What you are asking is impossible! Carmen has never lied. Nothing can change her mind. Everything is over between us."[31]

In contrast to Carmen, whose vision of love preserves the possibility of maintaining a distance between self and other, José incessantly, even obsessively repeats the phrases *je t'aime* and *je t'adore*—"I love you," "I adore you." Barthes argues that *je t'aime* is what linguists call a holophrastic expression.[32] That is to say: although it is composed of three words, its components come together when voiced as if they were only one. Indeed, the common French pronunciation of *je t'aime* as *j't'aime* reflects a sonic merging of these three words. The "I" (*je*) and the "you" (*te* or *t'*) disappear into each other, become each other, and fuse with *aime* (love). They are united, as it were, in love. *Je t'aime* is thus the perfect the verbal expression of José's possessive, narcissistic love.

José's aria in Act II, "La fleur que tu m'avais jetée," which recounts his days in prison and tells of his desire to see (*revoir*) Carmen again, is a poem composed of two parts, structured by the alternation of the first- and second-person pronouns (*je* and *tu*), either in the subjective or another case. The interchangeability of their positions is underscored by his starting with an object once belonging to Carmen, the flower, and ending with his own declaration that he is now her object: "And I was a thing belonging to you" (*Et j'étais une chose à toi*).

In prison, the smell of the flower he earlier received from Carmen triggers his memory, and José recalls her first appearance, her glance. Indeed, whether it is his mother (*Ma mère, je la vois*: "My mother, I see her") or Carmen who elicits his emotions (*Te revoir, O Carmen:* "To see you, oh Carmen"), for José the mechanisms of seduction and of love itself are always linked to sight. José sings of "his" days in prison, "his" thoughts, "his" desire. His aria seems less a cry of selfless surrender, as Paul Landormy would have it, than the expression of egotistic need, as McClary sees it.[33] Carmen is not blind to his words, "No, you don't love me," she tells him, "for if you loved me, over there, over there, you would follow me."[34] As Carmen senses, José's seemingly poignant expression of love is but an ode to himself. The fusion of the "I" and "you" in José's love is also apparent when he begs her to return to him: "Carmen, there is still time. Oh my adored Carmen, let me save you and save my-self with you."[35] In retrospect, one now understands the cigarette girls' attitude in the first act as they laugh at the young men's loving words and vows of passion, which they denounce as just so much smoke! In the second act, the Gypsies mock Carmen when she refuses to participate in their smuggling action by telling them that she is in love, madly in love. In the past, they remark, she was able to be in love and also to do her duty. But as she explains, this time love precedes duty, because she owes the soldier who has helped her. For her, to be in love is to partake in an economy, not of possession, but of exchange.

In the final act, the last word Carmen utters as she throws the ring, symbol of her relationship with José, back at him is *Tiens!*—which translates as "Here! Have it!" In French, this word is at the nexus of several intertwined meanings. First and foremost, before being endowed with any meaning at all, *Tiens!* is simply an exclamation, a cry, a sound, the bared expression of an emotion. Grammatically, *Tiens!* is the second-person imperative form of the verb *tenir*, which means *to have* or *to hold*. In French (as well as in English), in the imperative mood the personal pronouns—the exterior markers of the addresser and the addressee—are dropped. *Tiens!* thus appears as the link between an implicit "I" and an implicit "you." In returning the ring, Carmen thus gives back to José that which he has lost: the symbolic distance between "I" and "you," the space between his self and his mirror image. Finally, "Tiens!" recalls the closing lines of Carmen's Habanera: "you think you hold it, and it escapes you. You want to avoid it, and it holds you."[36] Remarkably, Carmen's final utterance blends his and her stories. Not merely a gesture of refusal, as Michel Cardoze suggests,[37] Carmen's final word is at one and the same time an assertion of freedom and a recognition of enslavement, both for herself and for José. In its explosive plurality, Carmen's last utterance is the ultimate signifier of her tragic love story, the trace of her understanding of love at once affirmed and denied, the graphic remains of her voice.

METAPHOR, METONYMY, AND THE BRICOLEUSE

"What is your name?" Escamillo asks. She answers: "Carmen, la Carmencita, as you please." Carmen presents herself with a formal first name and its intimate diminutive, but without the individualizing attribute of a patronymic. She thus presents herself as a spontaneous, self-generated being; someone essentially in the present without attachments to a historical lineage or a past. José, on the other hand, in response to lieutenant Zuniga's question as to whether he came from the Basque country, responds: "And of old Christian ancestry. My name is Don José Lizzarabengoa."[38] For José, identity is informed by geographical origin, religious affiliation, and social status (as denoted by *Don*, a marker of nobility). Most important, for him, the proof of his legitimacy is to be found in a family name. José's reply to Zuniga's simple inquiry even includes an explanation of why he left Navarre and how he became a soldier. While José's involved answer may have been necessitated in part by dramatic needs and constraints, it nonetheless grants him a precise identity defined by place, origin, time, and events. Identity for José has the structure of history; he is the incarnation of his personal history. For Carmen, identity is limited to the present and confined to an appellation by which she is—or wants—to be known.

In Andalusia, where the story takes place, a *carmen* is a villa or country house, a residence between culture and nature, belonging somehow to both, yet being part of neither—not unlike Bizet's heroine. In Latin, *carmen* means *song*, or poem, verse, prophecy, or incantation. As the etymology of her name implies, Carmen incarnates poetry, magic, and music, and she performs these arts—which are those of opera itself—with dazzling skill. At her arrest in Act I, she does not refuse to answer the lieutenant's questions, but merely gives him a non-answer, and with a simple "tra la la" dismisses his authority. Later, it is through a song, seemingly addressed to no one in particular, that she sets up a rendezvous with José at the tavern of Lillas Pastia. For her, only Tarot cards speak the language of truth; words are merely objects that can be fashioned to suit her purposes (Example 2.3).

In their itinerant lifestyles, the Roma were widely known at the time for their skills at mending household utensils, and they were referred to as tinkers. In some performances, Carmen is shown to break a plate in order to make castagnets.[39] She thus reveals herself to be what Lévi-Strauss calls a *bricoleuse*, a tinkerer—in other words, a Gypsy in every way.[40] A similar inventiveness characterizes her speech. When José tells her that he is repairing the chain of his priming pin—his *épinglette*—in Act I, she calls him *épinglier de mon âme*, that is to say, "fastener of my soul," an appropriate description of their story and a startling metaphor. Later, when José expresses his jealousy, referring simultaneously to his bile and his yellow uniform, she tells him that he is a "real canary in coat and character" (*Tu es un vrai canari d'habit et de caractère*). In this figure of speech, called a *zeugma*, two phrases or words belonging to separate registers are joined together: José's uniform with his jealousy, the concrete with the figural.

José, in contrast, is no *bricoleur*. In his world everything has a set function. His is what Lévi-Strauss calls the engineering mind:[41] he repairs a chain to restore it to its original purpose, keeps the file Carmen sent him to escape from prison in order to sharpen his lance, returns the money for which he has found no use. In comparison with Carmen's repertoire of rhetorical devices, José's verbal skills are noticeable only for their indigence. His speech is commonly prosaic. Whereas Carmen relies on a variety of tropes, the only figure of speech José uses is the simile. He tells us, for example, that Carmen's flower hit him "like a bullet"—a fitting image for his tragic story, but hardly an original image for a soldier. When he recounts the scene in the cigar factory, he describes Carmen "as rolling her eyes like a chameleon," adding that afterwards she was "sweet as a lamb." José's analogies are stereotypes: they do not add any new layers of meaning but simply intensify and elongate. They are merely syntagms of contiguity, and their function is metonymic.

Carmen and José share a predilection for animal imagery. But whereas in José's speech such images are comparative clichés, in Carmen's animals appear as metaphors. In the Habanera, she calls love "a rebellious bird"; to describe their relationship, she uses a proverb: *Chien et loup ne font pas longtemps bon ménage*—meaning, "Dogs and wolves do not cohabit together for too long." Such metaphors and metonyms are reproduced in Carmen's and José's arias about love. For her, love is expressed through a Habanera, a dance, the enactment of a movement; for him, desire is represented by the flower she once wore, an extension of herself, now belonging to him. In the final act, metaphor and metonymy are brought together visually and musically on stage, when José kills Carmen against the backdrop of a bullfighting arena.[42]

Metaphor and metonymy, the very stuff of literature, comprise one more set of dichotomies in the long inventory of oppositions that structure Bizet's opera. Besides the male/female and master/slave oppositions, or the metaphor/metonymy diptych, one could also, for example, discuss other seemingly adverse thematic networks: freedom in conflict with possessiveness, stereotypical northern ethics in contrast to southern mores, Spaniards versus

Gypsies, bourgeois values in collision with bohemian lifestyles. From a feminist perspective, one could easily denounce Bizet's opera as yet another work proclaiming that a woman's expression of her desire, her sexual pleasure, has to be stifled.

Or, one could hail Carmen for being a recalcitrant Echo to José's Narcissus. And one could regard any of these oppositions as subsisting in a dialectical process, in the hope of arriving at some synthesis that would erase all differences. More interestingly, at least for me, is the question of how to present a feminist reading of *Carmen* that does not limit itself to a mere reversal of oppositions but alludes to the possibility of some deconstructive displacement. By following Carmen's moves, by being attentive to her speech and listening to her voice, I have sought to make her words my own, I have abducted her language and tinkered with her love. Like Carmen's dual name, *Carmen* and *la Carmencita*, my readings of José's and Carmen's stories are not in opposition, but in apposition, set side by side, echoing each other. A zeugmatic process that joins the concrete with the figural, the metonymic with the metaphorical, the masculine of the text with its feminine, its exteriority with its interiority.

MYTHS AND SPECTATORS

For many commentators, the story of *Carmen* is only that of José; as one of Bizet's biographers, Winton Dean, once declared, "José is the central figure of Carmen. It is his fate rather than Carmen's that interests us."[43] In this view, a woman's presence, her experience, her emotional and sexual independence, are precisely what is unimaginable and in the end intolerable, as Carmen's fate will prove.

In answer to an interviewer's question insinuating that Bizet's heroine bears a strong resemblance to Don Juan and might be thought of as the female equivalent of Mozart's *Don Giovanni*, the singer Teresa Berganza—who created one of the memorable Carmens on the operatic stage—answered: "It's insulting to Carmen; it's also underestimating Mozart and misunderstanding Tirso's myth. Don Juan is a libertine ('Dissoluto punito'). Carmen is a liberated woman."[44] A philandering rake who kills an outraged father and then, in a scornful gesture of defiance, invites the statue of the dead commander to a banquet, Don Giovanni is a man who disdains social customs. His contempt for death seals his fate; he is condemned to an afterlife of suffering in Inferno. The perceived similarities between the working Gypsy and the playboy are in fact quite superficial. Where Don Juan is defiant of death, Carmen accepts death as the price to pay for her freedom. Both have more than one lover, but whereas Don Juan woos several women simultaneously, Carmen moves from lover to lover sequentially. In the second act, she tells Escamillo that he can love her as much as he likes, but "as to my loving you, just now that's out of the question."[45] A consummate seducer, Don Juan is the man of the broken promise.[46] Carmen, on the contrary, is proud to honor her word. "I pay my debts," she proclaims as she welcomes back the soldier who went to jail for aiding her escape, "that's Gypsy law, I pay my debts. I pay my debts."[47]

Yet, despite these significant divergences, commentators have often persisted in characterizing Carmen as a female

Don Juan.[48] It is as if she could not be accepted as *sui generis*. And yet, Carmen needs no model, she can simply be herself. This does not preclude a possible influence on Mérimée of the Don Juan myth. Ever since Molière's *Dom Juan* play of 1665, the legend has constituted an integral part of French culture. More pertinently perhaps, ten years before the publication of Mérimée's *Carmen*, Louis Viardot published in 1835 a study on Spain where he erroneously claimed that Tirso de Molina's Don Juan Tenorio was a relative of Pedro the Cruel (1334–1369), king of Castille, and his companion in debauchery.[49] At the time he was writing his *Carmen* novella, Mérimée was simultaneously working on a history of Pedro the Cruel. The Carmen–Don Juan comparison, while unconvincing, is certainly fortuitous.

Adorno argues that opera is intrinsically bound up with myth, because in opera "music intervenes in and transforms fate's blind, inescapable ties to nature (as they are represented in Western myth)—and the audience is called upon as a witness, if not indeed as an appellate court." But opera is also for him the site of a struggle between bourgeois values: "This interlocking of myth and enlightenment defines the bourgeois essence of opera: namely, the interlocking of imprisonment in a blind and unselfconscious system and the idea of freedom, which arises in its midst." What Adorno calls "the bourgeois essence of opera" is the interlocking of myth and anti-myth, blind destiny and the struggle for freedom, played out also in a competitive duel between *la musica e le parole*, between music and words. Hence for Adorno, "the form of the anti-mythological in the libretti of the nineteenth century

GEORGES BIZET'S *CARMEN*

is, however, exogamy, just as on the other hand, and quite logically, Wagner, who delivered opera as prey over to myth, shifted incest to the center of the opera ritual." Bizet's *Carmen* appears then as the emblematic example of "bourgeois opera": "The girl without a father and mother is irresistible, everyone who steps into her circle wants to up and leave with her like Don José and the gypsy." Like all art forms, opera blends both overtly and covertly aesthetic considerations with cultural, sociological, and political ideology. For Adorno, "It is precisely because opera, as a bourgeois vacation spot, allowed itself so little involvement in the social conflicts of the nineteenth century, that it was able to mirror so crassly the developing tendencies of the bourgeois society itself."[50] As "a bourgeois vacation spot," opera does not present to its audience bourgeois values per se; rather, it represents those values as violated or suspended, on vacation as it were.

Along these lines, in her own presentation of Bizet's *Carmen*, McClary calls our attention to the setup used to frame and direct the spectator's vision and understanding:

> Even if they [the soldiers] are ostensibly a Spanish army, they are of a significantly different class and ethnic constituency. They derive pleasure from gazing at the Other from positions of social privilege. In this, they resemble the audience. The opening number expressly legitimates distanced, objective, voyeuristic observation as we viewers are invited likewise to gaze unabashedly at "these odd people." Without necessarily noticing how, we enter into the opera's dramatic events from the soldiers' point of view. They naturalize spectatorship and situate us with the dominant social group that watches with amusement the colorful antics of the gypsies from the sidelines.[51]

In this decidedly nineteenth- and twentieth-century bourgeois optic, Carmen is indeed depicted as an exotic vamp, an inferior and treacherous being. In short, she is a danger to society.

In his study of love in the Western world, Denis de Rougemont attributed Western infatuation with passionate love to "oriental" temptation. With Christianity, he argued, marriage became a sacrament, and as such was founded on fidelity and fulfilled through procreation. Passion, on the other hand, as exemplified by the story of Tristan and Isolde, appears as a kind of mystic narcissism, where transcendence is no longer a means of elevation toward God but a negative sublimation of the self into death.[52] Passion and marriage are thus incompatible, in Rougemont's view. Accordingly, from this perspective, Western societies have endangered marriage by romanticizing passion. Yet as Adorno and many others have pointed out, marriage in the Western world is founded on exogamy, of marrying outside one's family or community group. The issue then becomes how to reconcile this need for exogamy with society's tendencies toward maintaining adherence to traditional values. Bizet's opera illustrates precisely this difficulty. Micaëla is the insider, the incarnation of bourgeois values, while Carmen, the outsider, an embodiment of sexual attraction, is perceived as a threat to the established order.

BIZET AND REVOLUTION

Musicologists have long puzzled over Bizet's desire to adapt Mérimée's novella for the operatic stage.[53] For historians of music the question is important: *Carmen* is one of the world's most popular operas, and it is considered Bizet's only masterpiece. "Were it not for *Carmen*," writes McClary, "Bizet's name would be no more familiar to us than those of his many contemporaries who were active in cultural productions at the time but who are now forgotten."[54] Bizet's determination, particularly in view of the obstacles he had to overcome to have such a story staged at the Opéra-Comique—a theater known as a place of domestic bourgeois respectability—made the composer's choice all the more perplexing. When Ludovic Halévy, who had been commissioned to write the libretto in collaboration with Henri Meilhac, informed Adolphe de Leuwen, one of the directors of the Opéra-Comique, of Bizet's project, the reaction was immediate:

> "*Carmen*! Mérimée's *Carmen*?" said Leuwen, "Isn't she killed by her lover?—And that background of thieves, gypsies, cigar-makers!—At the Opéra-Comique, a family theater! The theater where marriages are arranged! Every night five or six boxes are taken for that purpose. You will frighten off our audience.—It's impossible.[55]

Later, even as he authorized Bizet's project, Leuwen is said to have told Halévy, "Please don't have her die. Death, at the Opéra-Comique? That has never been seen! Do you hear me? Never! Don't make her die! I am begging you!"[56] In 1873, Bizet was in dire need of money as well as a success after the double failure of his *Djamileh* in May 1872 and *L'Arlésienne* in October of the same year. As the director of the Opéra-Comique pointed out, *Carmen* was a scandalous choice for a bourgeois audience, and Bizet was hardly one of those rebellious artists. On the contrary, he was described as dutifully middle class, an altogether good husband and good father. Indeed, in the words of his biographer Jean Roy, "There was in him no complacency towards the sordid."[57] Or in those of Michel Cardoze:

> A very ordinary man. . . . Hardworking moreover, without an ounce of adventure in life, in favor of the republic to keep things as they were, eaten up by house, family, and the conventional social relations that life had established around him.[58]

How, then, can we explain Bizet's attraction to Mérimée's story?

With respect to this question, Bizet's biographers have sometimes alluded to possible tensions in his marriage to Geneviève Halévy, first cousin of Bizet's librettist Ludovic. The Halévys were German Jews who had immigrated to Paris after the French Revolution. Bizet himself had studied music with Geneviève's father, Jacques Fromental Halévy, a recognized composer whose opera *La Juive* (1835) was performed throughout the nineteenth century. Set in the fifteenth century in Constance, *La Juive* stages issues of love, identity, and religious intolerance. In this respect, its themes are not far removed from those in *Carmen*, but in *La Juive* it is the young woman who leaves her family. Significantly, Roma and Jews have often been associated as "foreigners" in the popular imagination, and they have often shared the same fate. In Mérimée's novella, when the narrator-traveler first meets Carmen, she asks him to guess her ethnicity, and in this short seduction scene he enumerates the following possibilities—Andalusian, Moresque, Jewish—before she tells him that she is a Gypsy.[59] However, whether or not one can attribute Bizet's interest in the novella to this complex set of circumstances remains a conjecture.

As a result of Napoléon I's campaign of Egypt (1798–1799) and the colonial expansion of 1830, images of the exotic Orient were immensely popular in nineteenth-century France.[60] Gounod had given into the *genre oriental* with *La Reine de Saba* in 1862; ten years later, Bizet had offered "une orientale" with *Djamileh*. Furthermore, despite the protestations of the Opéra-Comique's director, the presence of Gypsies on the French cultural scene was not a new phenomenon, the best-known instance being in Victor Hugo's very successful novel *Notre-Dame de Paris* (1830). At one point, Bizet himself had thought of writing an opera about Hugo's Gypsy heroine, Esmeralda. Five years before *Carmen*, in his opera *La jolie fille de Perth* (1867), Bizet had Gypsies appear in a ballet.

Other hypotheses concerning Bizet's choice of his subject have been suggested. For instance, Henry Malherbe has argued that in 1872–1873 the newspapers were reporting on cases of former Communards now being called to account for their actions, and these may have reminded Bizet of Napoleon III and the Commune.[61] In his early years, Bizet had been a supporter of Napoléon III, but the anticlerical composer soon became disenchanted with the dictatorial regime and clericalism of the Second Empire (1850–1870). Unlike Bizet, Mérimée was a strong supporter of Napoléon III and a highly visible habitué of the entourage of the Imperial family. Eugénie de Montijo, wife of the Emperor, was the daughter of the Spanish Comtessa Manuela de Montijo, one of Mérimée's longtime friends. In fact, it was Comtessa herself who actually told Mérimée the story of Carmen in the first place, as the author acknowledged in his correspondence.[62] Thus, Mérimée was a name publicly associated with the Second Empire. From this standpoint, Bizet's opera, which ostensibly tells the story of a well-meaning but naïve soldier beguiled by an enticing Spaniard, might well be understood as portraying the imperial couple of Louis-Napoléon Bonaparte and Eugénie de Montijo, and presenting an allegorized version of the history of the Second Empire that ends with the emperor's "ignominious" defeat in the Franco-Prussian war. Perhaps the incidental occurrence of Mérimée's death on September 3, 1870, and France's defeat by the Prussians in that same year, reminded Bizet of Mérimée's work. For a disappointed Bizet, *Carmen* was perhaps a way to vent his frustrations against the second Empire, and at the same time to fulfill his presumed wish to compose an Orientalist work. It may also explain Bizet's determination to have *Carmen* performed at the Opéra-Comique instead of at the Grand Opéra, the theater associated with the imperial family.

Reading letters written by Bizet during the months of the Parisian civil war, Cardoze was struck by Bizet's vivid descriptions of his flight from Paris to Compiègne, his recounting of how he and his family had watched the fires of Paris from the rooftops. He was also struck by Bizet's complete obliteration of the fate of the Communards from his correspondence. After reading Bizet's letters, Cardoze notes that "There is in him an unbelievable aptitude for not noticing traces of repression." And he adds: "Bizet's attitude is due, it seems to me, to two causes: one social, one political." Cardoze attributed the political reason for Bizet's seeming disdain of the Communards to his fear that the uprising might bring about a return of the Catholic Right and the monarchy. More important for my purposes is the argument Cardoze proposed for Bizet's personal abhorrence: "A social reason, a class reason, deeply embedded in him: a profound aversion to social activism, a real apprehension concerning the future when faced with these movements."[63] But Bizet's attitude, as Cardoze argues, was not strictly one born of collective anxiety: there was no doubt in Bizet's mind that the insurrection would be stopped, nor was there any apprehension on his part about his own future or position in the social order. Rather, Bizet's erasure of the bloody and brutal repression of the Communards might be traced, in Cardoze's view, to a personal fright, an internalized terror possibly caused by some event witnessed by Bizet at an earlier time during the preceding revolution, that of 1848.

Bizet was ten years old when military forces attacked workers in front of the Conservatoire near his home in 1848. It is possibly this memory of that earlier uprising that would replay itself in Bizet's abjection of the Communards in 1871. In a recent biography, Rémy Stricker lends credence to the theory that some of Bizet's inspiration in composing the opera was political: "*Carmen* would certainly not be what it is without the events of 1870–1871, without their repression also, perhaps."[64] In 1870, Bizet might well have been experiencing anew the fear of revolutionary events he first felt in 1848.

In her work on culture and trauma, Cathy Caruth explains the process of displacement that inhabits the traumatic experience:

The experience of trauma, the fact of latency, would . . . seem to consist, not in the forgetting of a reality that can hence never be fully known, but in an inherent latency within the experience itself. The historical power of the trauma is not just that the experience is repeated after its forgetting, that it is only in and through its inherent forgetting that it is first experienced at all. And it is this inherent latency of the event that paradoxically explains the peculiar, temporal structure, the belatedness, of historical experience: since the traumatic event is not experienced as it occurs, it is fully evident only in connection with another place and in another time.[65]

In short, the experience of trauma forges (in two meanings of the word, i.e., moves forward and imitates) a hospitable venue for its delayed expression in a space and time other than the one that bore the imprint of the initial, and possibly forgotten, trauma. The trauma is caught, as it were, in a black box or echo chamber, a space that reproduces the event at a different moment and a different place. Another critic, Gertrud Koch, summarizes the latency and displacement occurring in the aftermath of a trauma this way:

The somatic impact of the traumatic shock . . . eludes all communicative expression of memory as a conscious process. . . . It is superceded [sic] by a form of staging as the recurrence of the experience. The traumatic incident is replayed, restaged, represented, either on the historical stage or in a reconstructed space.[66]

There is a curious letter from Bizet to an unknown correspondent dated by the editor simply as "written in 1870." Bizet writes, "This morning my neighborhood was invaded by the police. These civil servants stopped traffic, manhandled passersby, arrested those who asked questions, etc. I know that is necessary to maintain order, but it was strange (*inouï in Bizet's letter*) [*inouï in French* means "something unheard"] how today order resembled disorder."[67] For Bizet, the sight of the police forces roughing up civilians was transmuted into a sound effect, albeit an unheard one: something "inouï." In Bizet's letter, *l'inouï* becomes the symptomatic marker of a paradoxical moment, a moment of incomprehensibility, when opposites appear the same, when civil order and civil disorder are indistinguishable, indiscernible, from one another. In *Carmen*, one witnesses a similar reversal: in the first act, the soldiers impose order; in the second act, the Gypsies do. José is a representative of the law who becomes an outlaw, and the lawless Carmen prides herself on being a woman of honor who pays her debts.

It may not be entirely incidental that Carmen and José never join their voices in unison in a love duet. Not only are they psychologically ill-suited for each other, but they are mismatched culturally and socially as well. In other words, their union cannot be articulated, precisely because it is a shocking, unheard coupling, the impossible getting together of opposites. Carl Dahlhaus speaks of "a dark center" at the core of Bizet's opera, at the place of the absent duet between the protagonists, a muted space that signals a paradoxical moment, the simultaneous emergence of oppositional stances.[68] This unheard moment, this *inouï*, becomes the black box that may open for the listener a path of introjection and projection, allowing for the play of reversals and displacements, and the process of attraction and repulsion.

Stricker points out that *Carmen* is one of the rare operas, along with Mussorgsky's *Boris Godunov* and Puccini's *Turandot*, to feature the "people" on a par with the hero.[69] In Bizet's opera, the Gypsies are a jovial community of smugglers, not the sinister force of the underworld that we will see in Mérimée's novella. By depicting Gypsy outlaws as a community interacting amicably with the soldiers, who are the keepers of the law, Bizet presents a multi-ethnic peaceful society.

Placed between Carmen and José, facing the empty space between opposites, the spectator of Bizet's opera occupies the space of the backslash between dichotomies. The spectator, a witness to the drama, is implicitly interpellated as the third party, the judge in the dispute. Consciously or not, the spectator identifies with one, or the other, or both of the protagonists, and thus partakes in the struggle enacted onstage. At the end of the opera, while the story has as its denouement in Carmen's death, no possible solution to their tragic fate is offered. Unlike other operatic plots, where lovers must resist, overcome, or bow to the laws set down by oracles, emperors, kings, or fathers, in *Carmen* no external force intervenes between the protagonists, hence each of them bears full responsibility for his or her own fate. Whether it is dying for love in José's case or dying for freedom in Carmen's, Bizet's opera proposes itself as a poignant vision of the human condition, its pathos located at the juncture that marks the irreconcilable differences between its characters. Dependence versus freedom, loss of self in opposition to self-affirmation, destructive passion as opposed to free love, these are the themes of Bizet's masterpiece. As we will see, these sites of anguish are also embedded in Mérimée's short story. And it is precisely in the manner in which they are deployed or understood that each version of the Carmen story partakes in the unconscious of the myth.

FOR THE LOVE
OF SCIENCE

O N OCTOBER 1, 1845, Mérimée's *Carmen* appeared in
the *Revue des Deux Mondes*. At this first publication,
the novella was composed of three chapters of differing
lengths; a fourth chapter would be added in a later publication. In the first chapter, the traveler-narrator, a Frenchman,
is on a field trip in Andalusia looking for an ancient battlefield. But the story he will tell us is how he met the notorious
bandit José Navarro, and how, by alerting him, he saved
him from falling into the hands of the law. In the second
chapter, the narrator recounts meeting Carmen, who reads
him his fortune, steals his watch, and, when her lover
appears, suggests killing him. But her lover is none other
than José, who in return for the traveler's earlier saving gesture, lets him leave unharmed. When the traveler returns to

Georges Bizet's Carmen. Nelly Furman, Oxford University Press (2020). © Oxford
University Press.
DOI: 10.1093/oso/9780190059149.001.0001

Córdoba, he learns that his watch, easily identified by the distinctive sound of its chime, has been found and that José is in prison awaiting death for its theft and other crimes. In the third chapter, the traveler visits José in prison on the eve of his execution. It is then that José tells him the story of his life, supposedly transcribed "verbatim" by the traveler, that is to say, narrated in the first person by José. José recounts his life and tragic love. It is this third chapter that is the source of the plot of Bizet's opera.[1]

Mérimée, born into a well-to-do family of artists, was a self-educated scholar of history, anthropology, and linguistics. He was known as a ladies' man and remained a confirmed bachelor. He traveled extensively in part to fulfill his obligations as France's Inspector General of Historical Monuments. A French translator of Pushkin, Turgenev, and Gogol, as well as the author of several short stories and plays, he was at the time of *Carmen*'s publication a recognized historian, essayist, and writer, actively involved in the intellectual and social life of Paris. His texts are known for their stylistic sobriety and realism, in contrast to the exuberant prose of his Romantic contemporaries. While succinct in its narrative development, *Carmen* is replete with footnotes that gloss the text. These are meant to help the reader by giving translations of the Romany vernacular or the meaning of Spanish names, to pinpoint geographical venues, or to bring forth ancient history. These marginal paratextual elements are not merely added information or a self-promoting display of authorial knowledge; their importance lies elsewhere, for as we will see, they subtly inflect our reading and understanding of the text. When José recounts his own story in the third chapter, the traveler-narrator again directs our reading of the narrative by adding two lengthy explanatory footnotes. Both refer to Don Pedro, King of Castile, on whose historical biography Mérimée was working at the time when he was composing *Carmen*.

In the first and longest of these footnotes, the traveler-narrator explains how a street of Seville got its name: Candilejo. It was named after a lamp held by an old woman who saw two men fighting a duel. She recognized the surviving man as King Don Pedro by the distinctive sound of his tread. The next day, when the chief of police reported the duel to the King, who had earlier decreed that duelists would be decapitated and their heads displayed where the duel took place, the King told him to apply the law. The chief of police, a man of great wit—so the narrator tells us—decapitated a statue of the King and placed the head in a niche on the street (29). Three elements of this anecdote will find an echo in Mérimée's story: (1) sound as evidence of identification, (2) wit and ingenuity as a means of salvation, and (3) responsibility deflected through the use of representation.

A few pages later, the traveler-narrator appends yet another footnote concerning King Don Pedro. Here we are told that the Queen of the Gypsies, the bewitching Marie Padilla, gave the King's wife, Queen Blanche of Bourbon, a belt made of gold. Whenever Don Pedro looked at the belt he saw live snakes, hence his revulsion at the sight of his own wife. In this anecdote, the Queen of the Gypsies bears responsibility for the King's sexual repugnance toward Blanche (51). The theme of this footnote will be echoed in Bizet's opera, where the power of the Gypsy diverts male sexuality from its "legitimate" path.

Mérimée's *Carmen* opens with a Greek epigraph attributed to the fifth-century satirist Palladas. It says: "Every woman is bitter as gall. But she has two good moments: one in the nuptial bed, the other at her death" (1). The epigraph is meant to be a quip linking the lexical proximity of *thalamos*, a bridal bedroom, and *thanatos*, death. *Carmen* begins with a display of erudition that is also an obvious indictment of women. But since the quote is attributed to an ancient author, it begs the question as to whether Mérimée and/or the story's narrators are condemning its misogyny or endorsing it.

In 1847, two years after its first publication, Mérimée's *Carmen* was republished along with two other novellas, *Arsène Guillot* and *L'Abbé Aubain*. It was then that Mérimée added a fourth chapter. That fourth chapter proposes itself as a compendium on Romany lore, an ethnological study of the customs and language of the Gypsies. Its addition turns an already complex narrative into an even more challenging text, for that text now presents itself simultaneously as a traveler's memoir and a scientific paper. As we will see, this fourth chapter adds a cryptic and also racist component to the obvious misogyny presented earlier in the novella.

Since there had been no negative reactions to the initial publication of *Carmen* in 1845, the addition of the fourth chapter two years later seems to have been strictly a matter of authorial choice. In regard to this addition, two schools of criticism have emerged among Mérimée scholars: those who disregard the last chapter, and those who seek to incorporate it into their readings. My purpose here will be to add yet another layer to this debate about the relevance and function of the scholarly treatise Mérimée appended to the love story of José and Carmen. For although this "scientific dissertation" on the Roma presents itself as a corpus of historical, ethnographical, and linguistic knowledge, it is also a commentary that imprints the stories of the traveler and José with a distinctly racist bias.[2]

LANGUAGE, KNOWLEDGE, AND SCIENCE

After the epigraph, the novella's first sentence is an indictment against geographers:

> I had always suspected that geographers were talking nonsense when they located the site of the Battle of Munda in the territory of the Bastuli-Peoni, near present-day Monda, about two leagues north of Marbella. My own theories about the text by the anonymous author of the *Bellum Hispaniense*, and some information I gleaned in the Duke of Osuna's excellent library, led me to believe that the memorable spot, where for the last time Caesar played double or quits against the champions of the Republic, was to be found in the vicinity of Montilla. (1)

The ostensible purpose of the traveler here is to locate the site of the civil war that opposed Caesar's army to republican forces. And his opening lines, as if reflecting the affinity between *thalamos* and *thanatos* in the Greek epigraph, point out that the name of the battle of Munda is in close lexical proximity to the name of the supposedly erroneous site, Monda. Thus, on very the first page of his novella, Mérimée has already called our attention twice to the relevance of lexical changes and displacements—not only as the source of witticisms, as in the substitution of deathbed for bridal bed in the epigraph, but also as a potential source of error. "While waiting for my dissertation to resolve once and for all the geographical problem which is holding all learned Europe in suspense," Mérimée's traveler mockingly claims, "I want to tell you a little story. It in no way prejudges the fascinating question of the site of the battle of Munda" (1).

At the start of the novella, the commonly used literary device of the travelogue sets up the possibility of a narrative within a narrative, of the traveler's recollection and the protagonist's story. However, the traveler-narrator's insistence on the irrelevance of the purpose of his trip to the story he will recount immediately becomes suspect. For as we will see, Carmen and the Roma represent a danger to the racial ideology that informs Mérimée's tale. Roma women are to be feared as women who distract men from the responsibilities conventionally assigned to their gender, and Roma communities may be seen as potential causes of civil hostilities or unrest.

The novella's introductory clause—"I had always suspected that geographers were talking nonsense"—not only points to a rivalry between fields of knowledge but links explicitly the issue of knowledge to the issue of speech. Thus *Carmen* begins as an investigation of the relationship between knowledge and its expression (*savoir* and *dire*), and hence of the connection of speech to truth, of expression to deception, of deception to science. If geographers do not know what they are saying, it is implied, the narrator surely does. To speak is to take a chance and to bear a degree of responsibility. This point is made clear in the concluding paragraph of the fourth chapter, when the narrator declares: "I will conclude with this opportune proverb: 'En retudi panda nasti abela macha. A closed mouth, no fly can enter'" (339). This proverb may be no more than

a pointed remark, an ironically pithy conclusion to an eru-
dite treatise on Roma mores, but it reflects also Mérimée's
well-known and anguished flirtation with mystification. At
the same time, these last lines present themselves as an enticing bait—albeit a dangerous one—for interpretational
groping. Like its analogue, the English fly, a fishing lure,
is also *une mouche* in French, a word a letter away from
une bouche: a mouth.[3] From the closeness of the sounds
in the Greek epigraph to the slippage between Monda and
Munda, Mérimée inscribes a subliminal force to language.

NINETEENTH-CENTURY "GYPSIOLOGY"

With the fourth chapter of *Carmen*, Mérimée entered into
contemporaneous debates concerning the Roma, and in
the context of these debates into discussions concerning
race and social hierarchies. In the nineteenth century, the
question of the origins of the Roma people, then called
Gypsies, turned into an agonistic contest among rival fields
of study, opposing geographers to historians and historians
to linguists. Against this backdrop, rather than answering
the question of the location of an ancient battlefield, the
opening paragraph of Mérimée's *Carmen* can be read as
delineating the battleground of hostilities between distinctive fields of academic discourse.

A nomadic society linked by an oral language, the Roma
were a particularly enticing focus of study in Mérimée's
day.[4] After all, for those French social thinkers who valued
landed property because it was thought to promote political
stability, and who supported primary education for boys as
a way of fostering a national identity, the Roma presented

an intriguing if not a vexing problem. Without the benefit of either real estate holdings or formal schooling, they nevertheless constituted a highly organized, stable society. Their origins were obscure, their language little known, and in spite of centuries of coercion toward integration, they succeeded in preserving their language and lifestyle as they traveled throughout Europe. Where historians and anthropologists attempted to elucidate their origins by studying their history, migration patterns, trades and social mores, it was a German linguist, H. M. G. Grellmann, who, in *Die Zigeuner* (translated into French in 1787),[5] demonstrated that they were of Indian descent by showing that the Romany language was etymologically rooted in Indic, and thus belonged to the family of Indo-European languages.[6] With the subsequent publication, in 1841, of George Borrow's *Zincali: Gypsies of Spain*, questions relating to the Roma came to be of significant interest for social scientists and Europe's educated public as a whole.[7]

Social scientists of the nineteenth century often equated language and race, thereby assuming, as anthropologist Judith Okely points out, that language was transmitted or learned through biological descent.[8] Thus the proposition of a common Indo-European linguistic origin brought with it the proposition, shocking at the time, of the possibility of a common genetic source, a single racial ancestry possibly suggesting a universal human family, where all the descendants of Adam were kin. In opposition to the notion of an Adamic genealogy, the prevalent scientific hypothesis for the ancestry of Western societies in the mid-nineteenth century was the suggestion that Europe was populated by descendants of numerous unrelated tribes that had migrated west from India. For adherents of this view, the Roma were taken to be the very model of such a distinct tribe. "It was as if," writes the historian Léon Poliakov, "the Europeans of the scientific era, freed from the conventions of Noah's genealogy and rejecting Adam as a common father, were looking for new and specific ancestors without discarding the tradition that located their origins in some fabulous Orient."[9]

In opposition to a universal monogenism, some social scientists proposed a polygenetic model of human descent. Philologists compared the lexicons and grammars of various languages, noting their changes over time and establishing new classifications and subgroups within the Indo-European languages that would more closely correspond to distinctive population groupings. In the nineteenth-century imagination, evolutionary adaptive changes were not necessarily signs of progress. In fact, in a kind of inverted Darwinism, evolution was often tagged as a sign of degeneration. As Okely points out:

> Some [Gypsiologists of the nineteenth century] believed in the notion of a united Indo-European race with a "real" language of which many European and Asian forms were considered to be mere fragmentations. Similarly, Gypsy language and the "original culture" have been located as things once intact in India. It assumed that Gypsies existed in India many centuries back as a "pure" group or separate society with language, customs and genetic structure hermetically sealed, until some "mysterious event" caused their departure from their mythical homeland. From then on they are said to have been "corrupted" in the course of migration and during contact with non-Gypsies.[10]

In his now infamous *Essay on the Inequality of the Races* (1854), Arthur de Gobineau—with whom Mérimée corresponded occasionally—was not as much concerned with the question of the supremacy of what he called the "Aryan race" (although that superiority is implied) as he was with protecting Aryan racial purity from contamination and the threat of "degeneration." The nineteenth century had an obsession with the spread of disease and the effects of contagion, an obsession that would be somewhat tempered by Emile Pasteur's medical discoveries in the second half of the century. But the fear of contagion remained a virulent paradigm for explaining social events and authorizing political action. In such a racial ideology, miscegenation became a capital crime precisely because it was viewed as an erosion of the intrinsic asset of a "race," the noblest one being the "Aryan race" represented in its highest purity by the German people. Along with the classification of so-called racial groups, nineteenth-century linguists set up a corresponding taxonomy of languages, such as Indo-Aryan within the Indo-European family. Notions of social hierarchies or hereditary privileges did not altogether disappear after the French Revolution of 1789; rather, they seem to have commuted into social, racial, and ethnic rankings. As the anthropologist Benedict Anderson remarks:

> The dreams of racism actually have their origin in ideologies of *class*, rather than in those of nation: above all in claims to divinity among rulers and to "blue" or "white" blood and "breeding" among aristocracies. No surprise then that the putative sire of modern racism should be, not some petty-bourgeois

nationalist, but Joseph Arthur, Comte de Gobineau. Nor that, on the whole, racism and anti-semitism manifest themselves, not across national boundaries, but within them. In other words, they justify not so much foreign wars as domestic repression and domination.[11]

If we are to believe the ostensibly scientific memoir that constitutes the fourth chapter of Mérimée's *Carmen*, such hierarchical class distinctions occurred among the Roma themselves. "Their complexion is very swarthy, always darker than that of the people among whom they live: hence the name *Calé*, blacks, by which they often refer to themselves," writes Mérimée (333). To which he adds a footnote: "I got the impression that, although they understand the term *Calé* well enough, the Gypsies of Germany dislike being referred to in this way. Their own term is *Romané tchavé*" (333). According to this footnote, it would thus appear that differentiation along the black/white divide is an expected, unquestioned, "natural" phenomenon, for it is a discrimination supported by the *Romané tchavé* (the men of Roma) themselves. Later, Mérimée explains that *Romané tchavé* is the source of the word *romanichel*, meaning Gypsy in Parisian slang (338), thereby subtly connecting the Gypsies to the Parisian underworld. Linguistic ownership and its dissemination are thus evidence of social changes. Indeed, the critic André Billy once described Mérimée's *Carmen* as belonging to a body of "underworld literature," *la littérature de la pègre*,[12] a literature depicting social deviants for the reading pleasure, or displeasure, of the middle class.

The languages spoken by different Roma communities, as Mérimée portrays them, likewise reflect a comparable scale of values. The narrator himself notices the superior purity of the Romany spoken by the Germanic Gypsies. "The German dialect seems to me much purer than that spoken in Spain, for it has preserved a number of primitive grammatical forms, whereas the Gitanos have adopted those of Castillan Spanish" (338). In other words, the southern Gitano dialect is a degraded form of an original northern language, the purer vernacular of the Germanic Gypsies being indicative of the superiority of the people who speak it. This superiority is also attested by the fact that, according to the author, "In Germany, the Gypsy girls are often very pretty, but beauty is a truly rare attribute among the Gitanas of Spain" (334). This north-south geographical scale of value is reproduced in the novella where a progressively downward slant marks the relationship between the protagonists, distinguishing the northern French traveler from the bandit José, who is Basque and thus from Northern Spain, and further from the "devilish" Carmen of Seville in the south.

As in all societies, there are distinctive communities among the Roma. José recalls this scene from Gibraltar:

> You find every kind of riff-raff there, from the four corners of the earth, and it's like the Tower of Babel, for you can't go ten paces along a street without hearing ten different languages spoken. I saw plenty of Gypsies, but I hardly dared trust them. We were weighing one another up—it was obvious that we were all crooked: the question was, whether we belonged to the same gang. (41)

Acutely aware of the connections between racial discrimination and social stratification, José tells the French traveler that he comes from a titled old Christian family and had hoped to make a name for himself in the military. For José, as for all the other characters, ethnic identity is an essential feature, the determining factor in the drama that unfolds. Throughout the story, Carmen proudly claims her ethnicity, "*Calli* she was born, *Calli* she will die" (52), she tells José as he is about to kill her. Twice she points out that José is not a Gypsy but a white man, that is to say, a *payllo* in Romany. As for the traveler, he has no trouble understanding that he himself is the object of a heated conversation between Carmen and José. "The word *payllo*, which recurred often, was the only one I understood," he tells us, and he adds, "I knew this to be the word the Gypsies use to refer to any man not of their own race" (15–16). In the end, José's explanation of the story's tragic dénouement suggests that racism played a part in his crime of passion. The last statement of his own narrative, all the more noticeable since it is the concluding sentence of the third chapter, is straightforward: "Poor child! The *Calé* are to blame, for bringing her up as they did" (53). Not only does this statement obliterate José's responsibility for Carmen's murder, but it does not even find fault with Carmen's personal conduct—she has suddenly turned into an innocent child, the victim of her people. In his final judgment, José places the blame for Carmen's death strictly on her Gypsy upbringing. Accordingly, Carmen dies not because of José's violent temperament or uncontrollable jealousy, nor was Carmen killed for anything she did. She died because of who she was, a Gypsy. José's murder, his crime of passion, turns out to be a racist hate crime as well (Figure 2.1).

Freud has taught us that jokes and witticisms are often the symptomatic evidence of our anxiety and our alienation to ourselves. In this respect, Prosper Mérimée's celebrated witticisms, *bons mots*, and *mots d'esprit* can be very telling. While working on *Carmen*, alluding to his adventures among the Gypsies, Mérimée wrote to his friend Vitet: "I spoke to them in the Spanish dialect, they answered me in the German dialect, and as Epistemon might say, I nearly understood."[13] A dangerous linguistic closeness!

RACISM, MISOGYNY, AND RESPONSIBILITY

Starting with the Greek epigraph, Mérimée's novella presents women as both pleasurable and dangerous for men. In the second chapter, the French traveler is in Córdoba describing

FIGURE 2.1 Clip from Peter Brook's stage production of *La tragédie de Carmen*.

GEORGES BIZET'S *CARMEN*

how women at nightfall bathe in the Guadalquivir river, while men attempt to discern the bathers from the street. "No man would venture to mingle with that company," explains the traveler. But at a distance, "with a little effort it is not difficult to imagine one is watching Diana and her nymphs bathing, without risk of incurring the fate of Actaeon"—who, according to legend, was metamorphosed into a stag by Diana for his act of voyeurism, and subsequently devoured by his own hounds (12).

Women are attractive but dangerous; they can put a man's life in danger. Hence, the importance of male bonding. In the novella such bonding happens at the very start, when the traveler and José meet each other in a canyon, a place with water, trees, and shade, a uterine-like spot where they share a meal and cigars. Later, when Carmen asks José to kill the traveler and he refuses because the traveler earlier saved his life, she becomes yet another link between them, making it possible for the two of them to identify with each other as men.

Projecting responsibility for one's own actions or condition onto the other, blaming the victim, is one of the psychological mechanisms of racist hatred, and it is also at the core of racist discourses. In Mérimée's story, responsibility is represented in divergent modes. It displays itself when José becomes the narrator of his own story and avoids confronting his own moral responsibility, blaming Carmen's Gypsy upbringing for her death. In an earlier episode in the novella, when José kills the lieutenant who accompanied Carmen to the abode where José awaited her, he describes the incident in the following manner: "As the lieutenant was pursuing me, I pointed my sword at him and he impaled himself on it" (34). Here again, it is the victim who is blamed.

Responsibility is also thematically present and assumed by the traveler who, after having alerted José to the fact that his guide has left the inn to disclose José's location to the authorities, he shares with the reader his musings:

> Had I not betrayed my guide, who was upholding the cause of law and order? Had I not exposed him to the risk of incurring a blackguard's vengeance? Yes, but what about the obligations of hospitality? Primitive notions, I said to myself; I shall be answerable for all the crimes this bandit goes on to commit. Yet can one dismiss as primitive that instinctive call of conscience which is resistant to all reasoning? Perhaps, in the delicate situation in which I found myself, it would not have been possible for me to escape without some self-reproach. I was still in a state of complete uncertainty when I saw half-a-dozen horsemen appear. (10–11)

The traveler, at the crossroads between competing social obligations and cultural codes, is seemingly anguished by the morality and unforeseeable consequences of his decisions. His decision to alert José is for him an "instinctive call of conscience," beyond rational explanation, and thus "primitive." Only at the end of the novella does José question one of his actions: "I spent a long time looking for her ring, and eventually I found it. I put it by her in the grave, together with a little cross. Perhaps I was wrong to do that" (53). Was he wrong to bury her with the ring she threw away and the cross in which she did not believe? Does he take responsibility for negating Carmen's desire to break their relationship and her belief in the Tarot cards rather than Christian salvation? Do José's words attest to a moment of confusion between his and her divergent sentiments? José's murder of Carmen exemplifies the love-hate ambivalence as the trigger of a crime of passion, as well as a hate crime. Psychoanalyst Daniel Sibony explains it succinctly: "The height of the 'racist' crisis is to kill the part of the other in oneself. It is to mutilate oneself."[14]

Critics have often noted the substitution of narrative voices between the second chapter, told by the traveler, and third, narrated by José. For Mérimée's biographer A. W. Raitt, "Don José's narration will thus be authenticated by the credentials of Mérimée himself, who at the same time absolves himself from responsibility for Don José's criminal aberrations."[15] In a letter written by Mérimée to the Countess of Motijo on May 16, 1845, the author claimed that in *Carmen* he was only recounting a story she had told him some fifteen years ago—and thus, like the traveler in his own novella, he attributes responsibility for his story to another.[16] In Mérimée's work, the traveler—like the author—remains detached, safe from the "evil" he studies, untainted by the other. The "scientific" observer remains a Frenchman throughout; in contrast to José, he avoids "going native."

LANGUAGE, SEDUCTION, AND POWER

"In a closed mouth, no fly can enter": with this Romany proverb Mérimée concludes the fourth and last—the "scientific"—chapter of *Carmen* (339). It calls attention to the mouth and the ingestion of food, that is to say, to the buccal cavity as the site of passage of both food and language. If sharing cigars and food with José or smoking a cigarette and eating ice cream with Carmen (12–13) may be innocuous acts, a conversation presents a more serious challenge. As José explains, one's maternal tongue is a powerful transmitter of affect: "Our language is so beautiful, señor, that when we hear it spoken far from home our hearts leap at the sound of it" (23). José falls in love with Carmen at the moment she speaks to him in Basque, just as he is escorting her to prison: "Whenever she spoke, I believed her—I couldn't help it. She spoke Basque atrociously, yet I believed her when she said she was from Navarre. You only had to look at her eyes, her mouth, and her complexion to tell that she was Gypsy. I was mad" (24). A few lines earlier, however, José stated that "Carmen had quite a fair knowledge of Basque" (23). Did Carmen speak Basque well or atrociously? This apparent contradiction appears as the symptomatic textual evidence of José's madness.

Language is a forceful instrument of seduction and power, and the Roma, said to be everywhere at home, were renowned for speaking many languages. "As you know, señor," explains José, "the Gypsies have no country of their own. Being always on the move, they speak every language, and most of them are equally at home in Portuguese, French, Basque, or Catalan. They can even make themselves understood among the Moors and the English" (23). As the story of Carmen and José illustrates, the Gypsies' fluency with language is precisely what makes them so dangerous. This, of course, stands in sharp contrast to the narrator's own impressive display of knowledge in foreign languages (French, ancient Greek, Latin, German, Spanish, and Romany), which endows him with authority and scientific clout.

Mérimée concludes his chapter on the Gypsies with what seems to be simply another display of erudition. "Whilst I am airing my scanty knowledge of the Romany language," he writes, "I must draw attention to a few slang words borrowed from the Gypsies by our thieves here in France" (338). With this remark, language is revealed as a measure of the contagious expansion of Gypsies into French society. The cultural obsession with social misfits and degenerates that one finds in nineteenth-century literature appears as the symptomatic manifestation of the political anxiety and siege mentality of the newly established French bourgeoisie. Literary and cultural critic Jean Borie explains the social climate at the time in these words: "The birth of an industrial proletariat, the frequent reminders of revolutionary upheavals, the obsession with criminality, contact with colonized people created the specter of a proliferating degeneration that turned into a real social pathology."[17] The Gypsies, as represented in Mérimée's story, are consummate liars, thieves, smugglers, outlaws, and highway robbers who kill merchants and tourists. As Jean Borie argues, the presence in Paris of urban misfits, not unlike those represented by Mérimée, was experienced by bourgeois society as a persistent danger:

With the establishment of bourgeois legitimacy at the start of the nineteenth century, a new savage is born. His emergence . . . signals a demographic change, the move to Paris of bachelor immigrant workers, floating, swelling the low-income ghettos in the heart of the city, feeding the bourgeois imaginary with phantasms of prowlers, murderers lying in ambush, endemic revolutions, underground plots undermining nice neighborhoods, the invasion of civilization by hordes of new barbarians.[18]

By revealing traces of Romany in the slang spoken by French thieves, Mérimée implies that the story he told of southern Spain was likewise relevant to Parisian readers of the 1840s.

The Parisian world of Mérimée's time was composed of diverse individuals whose lifestyles did not always accord with bourgeois values. Among them were sons of bourgeois society itself—students, aspiring artists and writers—who lived unconventionally. They were called bohemians, in reference to the Roma who came to France from Bohemia an area located in the Czech Republic. In her study, *The Fate of Carmen*, Evelyne Gould views Bizet's opera as a telling example of "imaginery scenarios of bohemia," that is to say an expression of countercultural forces in opposition to the bourgeoisie.[19] In a short story entitled "A Prince of Bohemia" (1840), Honoré de Balzac defined Parisian bohemians in this manner:

> Bohemia, as we must call the theory of life current in the Boulevard des Italiens, is made up of young men between the ages of twenty and thirty, all of them men of genius in their way; little known as yet, but to be known hereafter, when they are sure to be distinguished. . . . The one word "Bohemia" explains everything. Bohemia owns nothing, and yet lives on what it has. Hope is its religion, faith in itself its code, and charity is supposed to be its finance. All its young men are greater than their misfortunes; they are beneath prosperity, but above destiny. Always astride on an *if*, witty as the column of jests in a newspaper, they are gay as only debtors can be, and oh! They are as deep in debt as in drink! Finally, this is what I am leading up to, they are all in love, overhead and ears in love![20]

During their university years, many of these young men attached themselves to working girls, whom they abandoned when, after their studies, they returned to their ancestral homes to marry and start families. This was the generation of young artists depicted in Henry Murger's serialized novel *Scènes de la vie de bohème* (1847–1849), which would serve as the basis of Giacomo Puccini's opera *La Bohème* (1896). As a lifestyle of young people, the bohemian existence often entailed subsiding in sordid conditions. But its poverty was made bearable by the generational camaraderie among the rebellious sons of bourgeois society, and by the hope that fame was yet to come.

In stark contrast, the other "bohemia," the milieu of thieves, smugglers, and murderers in Mérimée's novella, was widely feared by the bourgeoisie. "Bohemia" is thus a term that refers to two different social realities; it denotes a generational group that is a marginalized part of the bourgeoisie itself, and also the Gypsies, the people of Roma, an ethnic community that was actually foreign to it. Known and unknown, familiar and foreign, liked and despised, appealing and feared. Like the traveler who is attracted to José and Carmen while also fearing them both, the reader is fascinated and horrified in turn by the story being told. But significantly, the story of *Carmen* unfolds at a safe distance. It is told by a Frenchman who got to know them, those others in southern Spain—over there, far away. Yet when the "Oriental," the Gypsy, the foreigner, the other comes to Paris, the presence of that other within can become a source of fear, a fear that turns into racist hatred.

In its structural and narrative displacements, Mérimée's *Carmen* reveals the traveler's inability to accept the other as similar or different from himself, not simply because his fears and desires are projected onto him or her, but because that other puts him in touch with the stranger within himself, the unrecognized, unacknowledged, and unavowed part of himself. The stranger within, the double, like the biblical story of the brothers Cain and Abel, is a paradigm of social hatreds, a model often used to describe the structure of racism. In this respect, the concern of Mérimée's traveler for identifying the site of Caesar's last battle is not insignificant, for it was the determining battle in a civil war, a war between Roman "brothers." The sonorous closeness of Munda to the supposedly erroneous site of Monda is likewise not without relevance to the themes developed in the novella. For throughout the story, the narrator calls our attention to sound as possible evidentiary fact: the distinctive sound of Don Pedro's tread, the ringing mechanism of the traveler's watch, the manner in which José pronounces his *s*'s, revealing that he is a native of Basque country rather than Andalusia. In short, sounds and oral expressions are forms of evidence just as sight is. They substantiate the traveler's story, the historian's proofs, and the linguist's propositions.

Mérimée's novella, which has so often been read as a curious piece of travel literature or taken simply as the illustration of a case of fatal attraction, can also be considered a document that is indicative of, and has contributed to, the social myths of the nineteenth century. In her study of the Spanish Gypsy, which she entitles a "European Obsession," Lou Charnon-Deutsch calls our attention to the deployment of a scientific racism in concert with the establishment of nation states. As she emphasizes, the Roma people were, and still are, among the most disenfranchised groups in the making of modern European nations:

> Nation building and nationalism have a direct impact on the way dominant groups construct marginalized ethnic groups simultaneously as diseased members of a body that should be if not amputated at least quarantined, or, conversely, as exotic assets to some imaginary pluralist society. With the waning of Enlightenment universalism that sought to transcend human differences, racial difference and inequality had to be explained by other means than mere cultural differences, and the result was a scientific racism that relied on empirical data to stratify populations. Science was called upon to explain the inequities and differences endemic in rising capitalist societies, and it obliged by explaining the Roma's social degradation by recourse to physiological inferiority. Ethnic identity in the modern sense is an offspring of the process of state formation; when nationalism is on the rise in a given state, issues of difference generally gain prominence, and ethnic myths proliferate.[21]

Under the cover of having a historical and scientific purpose, Mérimée's narrator becomes a witness testifying for José, his character, and the truth of his story. The novella demonstrates the ubiquitous, porous, boundless nature of cultural, scientific, and dominant ideological constructs. It illustrates the nineteenth-century belief in social and cultural hierarchies and values, and makes explicit the similarity of the psychological structures of racism and misogyny.

Bizet and the librettists Meilhac and Halévy avoided the obvious racism and misogyny of the novella by pegging the characters and other elements of their opera to a different system of values. Their Gypsies are not fearsome murderers; they are a friendly, joyful community of hard-working smugglers who fraternize with representatives of the law at the tavern of Lillas Pastia. They even save Lieutenant Zuniga from being attacked by José in the second act. The suggestion that the Gypsies are a dangerous alien community is thus erased in the opera. Gypsies are presented as a jovial and engaging group. Carmen is not the driven leader of a male band of smugglers and highway robbers and killers. She is a woman who enjoys the banter of the soldiers and the teasing of members of her Gypsy clan. Like José, she is a believer, but whereas he believes in the Catholic faith, she believes in the omens of the Tarot cards. In the opera, José is not quite the serial killer of the novella. By focusing the plot strictly on the love story, the opera eschews many of the racist components of Mérimée's story.

As we will see, while numerous films dedicated to Carmen portray her as a *femme fatale* or a combative ideological heroine, others embrace her story in order to depict and celebrate a number of distinctive, self-proclaimed ethnic communities. While many films turn to the novella for inspiration, these films offer a wide spectrum of reactions to the misogyny and racism salient in the Mérimée's story, each film reflecting or deflecting cultural prejudices and social taboos.

CHAPTER 3

SCREEN WOMAN

NEITHER THE CELEBRITY OF Bizet's opera nor the numerous readers of Mérimée's novella can account entirely for the extraordinary popularity achieved by Mérimée's heroine. Viewers of opera and readers of books are no match for the audiences reached by films, and the international appeal of Carmen on the silver screen has been phenomenal. The Carmen Project, created by a team of scholars at the University of Newcastle, published *Carmen on Film: A Cultural History*, which reveals that the story had spawned nearly eighty films by 2007.[1] Carmen has attracted an international roster of illustrious directors, among them Charlie Chaplin (USA), Cecil B. DeMille (USA), Jacques Feyder (France), Jean-Luc Godard (France), Ernest Lubitsch (Germany),

Georges Bizet's Carmen. Nelly Furman, Oxford University Press (2020). © Oxford University Press.
DOI: 10.1093/oso/9780190059149.001.0001

FIGURE 3.1 Charlie Chaplin, poster of film (USA, 1916).

Otto Preminger (USA), Joseph Gaï Ramaka (Senegal), Francesco Rosi (Italy), Carlos Saura (Spain), and Seijun Suzuki (Japan).

The early days of cinema, just before and during World War I, saw a cluster of cinematic Carmens. Chaplin produced *A Burlesque on Carmen* with a jazzed-up version of Bizet's score, a project that was intended to mock an earlier Carmen film by Cecil B. DeMille. DeMille's silent film had been shown at Boston's Symphony Hall as a major musical event, with Hugo Riesenfeld directing Geraldine Farrar of the Metropolitan Opera together with a full symphony orchestra, in a live performance to accompany the projection of the movie. During these same years, Ernest

FIGURE 3.2   Geraldine Farrar, poster of film by Cecil B. DeMille (USA, 1915).

Lubisch produced the silent German film *Gypsy Blood*, starring Pola Negri in Carmen's role.

In the United States, Raoul Walsh first directed *Carmen* in 1915, starring Theda Bara and Einar Linden, and then *The Loves of Carmen* in 1927, starring Dolores del Rio and Don Alvarado. This early flock of films may have been responding in part to anxieties created by the First World

FIGURE 3.3 Pola Negri, poster of film by Ernst Lubitsch (Germany 1918).

War (1914–1918) and America's ambivalence toward joining forces with the Allied Powers. For as we have seen, *Carmen* has often been understood as the story of a soldier caught between the call of duty and sexual attraction. These early films may also have responded to efforts of the suffragette movement for voting rights, which was a major international issue during the years leading to and following

World War I. For the Carmenologists of the University of Newcastle, these early films, as those that will follow in the 1980s have "two features in common: they appear at a time when women were becoming more independent, and at a time when the industry wished to attract middle-class audiences to the cinema."[2]

In 1933, German filmmaker Lotte Reiniger presented a nine-minute animated version of *Carmen*, produced with black cutout figures moving against a white backdrop accompanied by a montage of Bizet's score (Figure 3.4). Reiniger's film is unabashedly feminist; she interprets the story through Carmen's desire and vision by having Carmen realize her dream of riding away with her lover. In Act II of Bizet's opera, as José gets ready to return to the military barracks, Carmen tells him, "If you loved me, out there, out there you'd go with me! You'd carry me away on your horse and like a hero, you'd ride into the hills."[3] At

FIGURE 3.4 Clip from animation film by Lotte Reiniger (Germany, 1933).

the end of Reiniger's film, Carmen rides off with the tore-ador Escamillo on the back of a liberated bull, leaving José behind.

Films, especially when they offer an opportunity to show-case a seductive woman, are particularly suited to titillate spectators. As the film critic Laura Mulvey reminds us: "In their traditional exhibitionist role women are simultaneously looked at and displayed, with their appearance coded for strong visual and erotic impact so that they can be said to connote *to-be-looked-at-ness*."[4] This point is well illustrated in Charles Vidor's film *The Loves of Carmen* (1948) with Rita Hayworth, at the time one of Hollywood's most glamorous stars, who embodied feminine seductive beauty; she played opposite Glenn Ford, who was one of Hollywood's be-loved leading men. Because of the size of the screen and the spectators' closeness to the image projected, cinema offers an array of choices among visual pleasures: aesthetic delight, voyeuristic enjoyment, persuasion through visual recogni-tion, and identification; in short, satisfaction of visual desires.

Both in Mérimée's novella and in Bizet's opera, Carmen's entrance is carefully planned and orchestrated. In the short story, she comes out of the dark as the traveler-narrator is attempting to catch sight of the women bathing at dusk in the river. In the opera her entrance is prepared and announced by the chorus. In both, her appearance is framed to provide a focal point that makes her attraction and glamour seem natural, arousing the curiosity of readers and spectators. As the feminist theorist Laura Mulvey points out, the structure of sight is built around a double psychic mechanism: attrac-tion to the person being viewed and/or identification with that person. She writes:

The first, scopophilic, arises from the pleasure in using another person as an object of sexual stimulation through sight. The second, developed through narcissism and the constitution of the ego, comes from identification with the image seen. Thus, in film terms, one implies a separation of the erotic identity of the subject from the object on the screen (active scotophilia), the other demands identification of the ego with the object on the screen through the spectator's fascination with and recognition of his like. The first is a function of the sexual instincts, the second of ego libido. [...] But both are formative structures, mechanisms without intrinsic meaning. In themselves they have no signification, unless attached to an idealisation. Both pursue aims in indifference to perceptual reality, and motivate eroticised phantasmagoria that affect the subject's perception of the world to make a mockery of empirical objectivity.[5]

When viewing a film, the gaze of the spectator often becomes trapped in that of the lens of the camera. Whether the erotic charge is libidinal, narcissistic, or a convergence of the two, the Carmen we watch on the silver screen is the one seen by the camera, and most often the camera follows José's gaze. Hence most films on Carmen espouse José's viewpoint, look at Carmen through José's eyes, and thus tell only his story. Carmen incarnates the *femme fatale* as a projection of José's ego and object of his desire. This is consonant with the structure proposed in the opera, where sight is marked as masculine, as we observed in the soldiers' waiting to see Carmen, and in José's stated need to see Carmen again. On the other hand, music, dance and language, that is to say the acoustic elements, are marked as feminine. From this perspective, as we will see, the changes that Bizet's score experienced in its many filmic adaptations tell stories of their own.

OTTO PREMINGER'S CARMEN JONES (1954)

In Preminger's *Carmen Jones*, the music is composed of excerpts of Bizet's score mixed with pop or jazz to support Oscar Hammerstein II's lyrics, composed for a 1943 Broadway musical of the same title. Preminger's film is a decidedly American story, as the "Jones" in the title intimates. Located in rural Florida, it is the story of an African American soldier who, after killing his sergeant, flees with his beloved Carmen, a worker in a parachute factory, to seek a new life in Chicago. The film's opposition between opera on the one hand and Broadway musical on the other reflects cultural rankings that are in step with social hierarchies of the time, and thus their intermingling destabilizes accepted notions of high and low art forms. Harry Belafonte, who plays Joe in Preminger's film, explained:

> Because it was to be a black-cast movie, and because blacks were still exotic to Europeans—and the movie had to be a financial success in Europe as well—Otto [Preminger] had to find a way to please the Bizet estate, which did not like what Hammerstein had done to the original work. They felt turning Carmen into a folk opera was not servicing the best needs of the opera, so Otto appeased them by hiring two opera singers to dub the main voices.[6]

Whether the dubbing was a commercial necessity or not, this substitution of operatic voices for the then well-known voices of Dorothy Dandridge and Harry Belafonte introduces a noticeable and significant social and cultural change. In the film, when the jazz performer Pearl Bailey sings "Beat Out That Rhythm on a Drum," she becomes the voice of African American musical identity. This moment corresponds to the start of the Gypsy number at the beginning of the opera's second act. In Preminger's film, the soundtrack for the film conveys a clear political message. In the 1950s, opera was considered high art, and most opera singers were white.[7] Preminger presents spectators with the then-unusual sight of black bodies singing with voices culturally marked as white, in a strange sort of miscegenation. In Preminger's film, Joe does not stab Carmen as José does in both opera and novella. Rather, he strangles her in a janitor's closet. Not that Joe is incapable of stabbing someone; a moment earlier in the film we see him pull a knife on the character of Husky Miller in the gym. If one is to read the strangling of Carmen Jones as a metaphor for the film as a whole, then she dies not only because she has become Husky Miller's mistress, but also because she has sold out her black voice for a white one, with all the values inscribed in that exchange (Figure 3.5).

FIGURE 3.5   *Carmen Jones* poster of film by Otto Preminger (USA, 1954).

"ALL WOMEN ARE NAMED CARMEN": THE FILMS OF 1983

With three major productions, 1983 marked a blockbuster year for our heroine. Italian director Francesco Rosi filmed the opera on location in Seville; Carlos Saura, in collaboration with the choreographer Antonio Gadès, presented a Spanish dance version simply called *Carmen*; and the always impertinent Jean-Luc Godard shocked French audiences with his *First Name: Carmen*. In 1983, Mérimée's Gypsy became *the* screen woman of the year. All of these Carmens, filmed by major directors and appearing within a few months of each other, were newsworthy. As the French magazine *Le Nouvel Observateur* printed across the cover of its August 19 issue: "All women are named Carmen"—a statement that calls attention to the figure of Carmen perceived as the very incarnation of "woman."[8] Ann Davies attributes this cluster of Carmens in 1983 to the fact that the copyrights held by the librettists' families had finally lapsed, thus making it possible to claim Bizet's opera, as opposed to Mérimée's story, as the principal originating source of the films.[9]

Films, like other cultural artifacts, reflect the societies from which they emanate, and as the scholars of the *Carmen Project* point out, "the Carmen films are symptomatic of shifts in the condition of women."[10] The 1983 Carmens came at the close of a decade marked by fights for reproductive freedom and equal rights for women in France, Italy, and Spain, as well as the fight for the Equal Rights Amendment in the United States. It was also the decade when the "Iron Lady" Margaret Thatcher, prime minister of the United Kingdom, was the most visible, powerful, and controversial woman on the international political scene. The 1983 revivals inserted themselves into the feminist debates of these years, but they are more indicative of an anti-feminist stance than supportive of women's rights and independence.

FRANCESCO ROSI'S *BIZET'S CARMEN*

Of the three films produced in 1983, only Rosi's remains faithful to the opera's score and libretto. Conducted by Lorin Maazel, with Julia Migenes-Johnson playing Carmen, Plácido Domingo as Don José, Faith Esham as Micaëla, and Ruggero Raimondi as Escamillo, Rosi's version of Bizet's opera is not a filmed theater production but a cinematographic one, produced on location in Andalusia. The director of a highly acclaimed 1964 motion picture on Spanish bullfighting, *The Moment of Truth*, Rosi returned to this theme by framing Bizet's opera in the visual trope of the *corrida*. By choosing the bullfighting arena as the privileged site (place) and sight (viewpoint) of the story and its telling, Rosi produced a Carmen that, in view of many critics, both met and exceeded expectations. In view of these acclaims, the hackneyed, commonplace metaphor of the bullfighting arena surely demands to be further examined (Figure 3.6).

From its very start, the sights and noises of the arena fill the screen and the soundtrack of Rosi's film. Bizet's overture begins at the very moment when the *espada* of the matador kills the bull; while the body of the bull is removed, the matador is carried around the arena to the acclaim of the public. The music breaks off, and the film cuts away to a nighttime religious procession, led by hooded figures of

FIGURE 3.6 Clip of bullfighting arena from film by Francesco Rosi (France/
Italy, 1984).

penitents holding crosses and candles and carrying a statue
of the Virgin Mary. As the procession passes, Bizet's overture resumes and ends. At the conclusion of the film, the
arena once again becomes the focus of Rosi's camera. There
is the main arena, where Escamillo will be cheered by the
crowd, and just off the main arena a smaller one, where
Carmen will find death at the hand of José. During the last
sequence, shots of the bull and the matador that opened the
film reappear at intervals.

Not one but three bullfighting arenas therefore appear in
Rosi's film: the referential *corrida* that features the actual
killing of a bull, the backdrop arena that serves as the theater
of Escamillo's success, and the arena where Carmen meets
her fate. These three arenas constitute a signifying chain
of interchangeable spaces, subverting their oppositions,
collapsing analogical distance into structural indifference,

substituting sameness in lieu of difference. In Bizet's opera, Escamillo's arena serves as an analogy. It provides a figurative likeness to José's killing of Carmen, and at the same time places Carmen between two arenas representing her life: that of José's murderous passion, and that of her relationship with Escamillo. The theatrical backdrop provides dramatic intensity to Bizet's fourth act, but leaves the audience free to interpret the bullfighting arena from either José's or Carmen's perspective. In contrast, by opening, framing, and enclosing his film with such vivid images of the bullfighting arena, Rosi leaves no room for Carmen's story—the story of a woman caught between what was and what could have been. Rosi interprets Carmen's death as a sacrifice equal to the sacrifice of a bull for public enjoyment.

Scholars of the arts have taught us to be suspicious of "realism," whether in literature or in the visual arts. In making things appear "natural," hence "truthful," realism transmits immediately understandable visual images, using them but not necessarily contesting them. Whereas Bizet's opera creates a distance between the killing of a human being and the ritual slaughter of an animal, Rosi displays these two events as similar and contiguous. From the religious procession in the opening of the film to the sight of the matador praying before entering the arena, elements combine in Rosi's film to present the *corrida* as an event under religious supervision, a ritualized sacrificial occasion. In framing Bizet's opera in this sacrificial perspective under the aegis of the Church, not only does Rosi embrace José's viewpoint, but he also proposes Carmen's death as a sacrificial offering condoned by the Church. Far from being

Bizet's Carmen, as the title of Rosi's film leads us to believe, Rosi's rendition of the opera is very much his own.

"The bull sees red," writes Roland Barthes, "when the lure gets under his nose; the two reds—that of his anger and that of the cape—coincide; the bull is in an analogy, that is to say fully in the imaginary."[11] For Barthes, the word "imaginary" refers to understanding images and language as always culturally mediated and thus not as transparent, unquestioned truths. Under the guise of making a "realistic" Spanish Carmen, Rosi presents us with the story from José's viewpoint, where Carmen remains caught in José's *Weltanschauung*. He perpetuates the fantasy or fallacy (more precisely perhaps the *phallacy*) that Carmen is a victim deserving her own victimization. Jeremy Tambling reads Rosi's bullfighting "as a symbol of a male power at work in the film," and José's killing of Carmen as "the defence of a male power that has lost its ability to quell in other ways."[12]

Throughout Rosi's film, the acoustic narrative carries the sounds of life depicted on the screen: the cries and applause of spectators of the *corrida*, the noise of people talking, the sounds of the horses and mules. For H. Marshall Leicester Jr., the "noise track represents everyday unselfconsciousness," whereas Bizet's music, and most particularly the singing, "register[s] self-conscious moments." Leicester thus credits Rosi with having found "a code that allows him to map the interplay of emotions" of the protagonists.[13] During the second act in Rosi's adaptation, in which José and Carmen first meet as lovers in Lillas Pastias's tavern, "there is," Leicester remarks, "a steady rhythmic drone of crickets," which disappears when José starts singing the "flower song," only to reappear and then disappear again when Carmen sings her aria, "Non, tu ne m'aimes pas."[14] More than the emotions imputed to the protagonists, the drone of the crickets provides a static noise that marks the vocal exchange between them as an acoustic buzz, a miscommunication. This droning of crickets, this parasitic hum, is precisely that which re-presents audibly the distance that separates Carmen from José, and the irreconcilable differences between Bizet's protagonists. The originality of Rosi's film resides in its acoustic narrative, in this static noise between the lovers' arias, and thus in its understanding of Bizet's *Carmen* as the staging of an impossible coming together, the drone of the crickets suggesting the incommensurable, essential loneliness of the protagonists, even as they partner in love.

CARLOS SAURA'S *CARMEN*

Carmen is the second in a trilogy of flamenco dance films directed by Carlos Saura. *Bodas de Sangre* (*Blood Wedding*, 1981) was the first, and *El Amor Brujo* (*Love the Magician*, 1986) the last. In Saura's rendering, produced in collaboration with the choreographer Antonio Gadès, the story of *Carmen* concerns the creation of a ballet in the flamenco tradition (Figure 3.7). The film credits appear against a sepia-colored photo of the dancers. Most of the film takes place in a modern dance studio, its walls covered with mirrors, with a wall-length window looking out onto the street. Saura filmed the ballet by setting the camera at the height of the dancers' ankles and moving it along the stage, capturing images of the dancers from different angles and showing their reflection in the studio's mirrors. When the film starts, we see a woman sitting at a table singing a Gypsy song accompanied by a guitar player. Then the camera focuses on Gadès as he listens to Bizet's score on tape. When Gadès plays the recording of the "Seguidilla," the guitarist Paco de Lucia points out that it would be difficult to dance to the opera's music, and he replays it with flamenco rhythms as a *buleria*. In Saura's *Carmen*, Bizet's score serves as a foil against which to highlight and showcase "real" Spanish music and dance. This first scene capture the essence of the film: a rivalry between Spanish flamenco and Bizet's French intimation of Spanish music. The blurring of reality and art is indicated by the see-through wall of the dance studio; the reflected movements of the dancers in the mirror, suggesting self-reflexivity; and the relationship of the past to the present, hinted at by the old sepia photograph of flamenco dancers at the start of the film. With his *Carmen*, Saura continues—the efforts by two Spanish cultural icons, the writer Federico García Lorca and the composer Manuel de Falla, whose work brought Andalusian music and dance back to the fore, as genuine high art.

Gadès, the guitarist Paco de Lucia, and the dancer Cristina de Hoyos, all of whom are highly acclaimed performers, appear as themselves in the film. Carmen is played by Laura del Sol, a younger dancer whom the more experienced Hoyos is asked to train. The competition between Bizet's classical music and flamenco rhythms is but one of several rivalries in Saura's film. The rivalry between Carmen's husband Garcia and José is inspired by Mérimée's text, but the competition between a younger Carmen and an older woman is not to be found in either the novella or

FIGURE 3.7   Clips from film by Carlos Saura (Spain, 1983).

the opera. The film intermingles the love story of Carmen and José with another love story: between the "real" Gadès, who plays José, and the "real" Laura del Sol, who plays Carmen. Art and reality, ballet and life, are fused. They are indistinguishable from each other, just as the studio's glass wall opening onto the street suggested.

Gadès, a middle-aged dancer shown stretching a painful shoulder, is conscious of the passing of time. The return of flamenco music in the film likewise prompts reflections on the past: specifically, the awakening of Spain from the Fascist dictatorship of Francisco Franco, which lasted from 1939 until 1975. Saura's trilogy was produced during the transitional period marked by the return of King Juan Carlos I, heir to the throne of the Bourbons, the instauration of a democratic government in 1978, and Spain's entry into the European Union in 1986. Through its visual clues and musical rhythms, Saura's *Carmen* proclaims an autonomous cultural identity for Spain on a par with those of other European nations.

One of the leaders of the influential French New Wave Cinema of the 1960s and 1970s, Godard is a notorious film critic, famed film director, and outspoken Marxist intellectual, adulated by many and excoriated by some. There is, however, agreement among all that his relentless questioning of conventional film structures, from image to sound to narrative development, has been highly influential. The release of any Godard film is an event eagerly awaited by fans of his conceptual innovations, and also by the merely curious for the potential shock value of his films. *First Name: Carmen*, which received the Golden Lion for Best Film at the 1983 Venice Film Festival, did not disappoint. It has a disconcerting narrative, disjointed images and sounds, and a large number of visual and verbal puns, and it is replete with aphorisms and cultural references. In addition, Godard had the audacity to show male and female frontal nudity, as well as Joseph (named for José) masturbating in an attempt to have an erection. Moreover, by substituting movements of Beethoven's string quartets for Bizet's music, Godard, always the brazen iconoclast, thumbed his nose at one of France's best-known cultural creations.

First Name: Carmen presents itself as a film within a film. The first film stars Godard himself as Uncle Jean, and serves as a frame for the second film, the film within, which takes up the story of Carmen. In the first film, Uncle Jean is in an insane asylum, where he is visited by his niece, Carmen, who asks if she can use his beach house to make a film. Carmen, played by Maruschka Demeters, is a young and attractive woman, hardly a sultry vamp. Her film is about a robbery that will lead to a political kidnapping. The robbery is filmed in a farcical mode, a grotesque presentation that may hark back to Chaplin's *A Burlesque on Carmen*, for Godard's film ends with the words, "In memoriam of small films written on the screen," and Carmen also makes reference to Otto Preminger's *Carmen Jones*, when she refers to Joseph as Joe and quotes Carmen Jones's line in English: "If I love you, that's the end of you." The main character in this inner film sequence is not Carmen but Joseph, played by Jacques Bonnaffé. He is a man rejected by all: the police, the head of the gang, and, of course, Carmen. Socially washed up, his virility gone and abandoned by his lover, Joseph incarnates a man in crisis, emasculated and powerless. Michaela makes a fleeting appearance; she is played by Claire, a member of the string quartet that provides the musical background for the film. A nurse, first seen in the asylum writing down everything the doctor says, reappears at the end as a script girl writing down every word Uncle Jean utters. Women, it seems, can play interchangeable roles and can be substituted for one another. They can all be named Carmen.

The first film, the one within which the Carmen story takes place, features Uncle Jean as a deranged filmmaker (Figure 3.8). He shows his new camera, a large tape recorder he holds against his ear, and says, "We should close our eyes, not open them." Clichéd visual metaphors appear on screen: sea waves to denote lovemaking, trains passing each other in the night to indicate misunderstanding or missed opportunity. Holding a tape recorder instead of a camera, Godard plays a deranged filmmaker bearing his

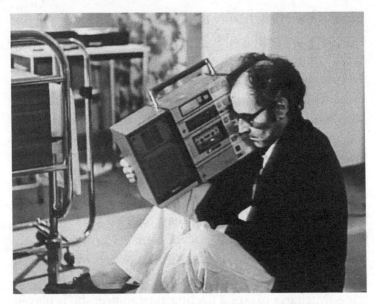

FIGURE 3.8 Clip of film by Jean-Luc Godard (France/Switzerland, 1984).

own first name in an ostensibly parodic, self-depreciating autobiographical gesture.[15]

A few bars of Bizet's Habanera are heard twice in the film: whistled first by a man in the asylum and later by a young man in a café. Music is made visible throughout with shots of the quartet rehearsing Beethoven's composition. Throughout his film, Godard calls attention to the differing paths of the moving images and the soundtrack, as two distinct forms of narrative, telling different stories. In *First Name: Carmen*, some of the visual images and words refer to film history and propose a remake of the Carmen story, whereas the soundtrack, by rejecting Bizet's music in favor of Beethoven's, may indicate that it could only have been filmed by a madman, or perhaps a genius.

AN ICON FOR A NEW MILLENNIUM

The 1983 films by Rosi, Saura, and Godard speak to the social, political, and cultural concerns evident at the end of the twentieth century, especially women's struggle for reproductive rights and other personal and professional ambitions in a "second-wave feminism" that was widely perceived as threatening to men who felt robbed of their inherited patriarchal rights. In contrast, film adaptations of the early 2000s endow Bizet's heroine with a whole new set of features, motives, and actions. Robert Townsend's *Carmen: A Hip Hopera* (2001), Joseph Gaï Ramaka's *Karmen Geï* (2001), and *U-Carmen* from the Dimpho Di Kopane theater company (2005) offer exhilarating renditions of the Carmen myth, all played by black performers. These films speak of racism and misogyny in unexpected ways. No longer the provocative vamps of early cinema nor the dangerous seductresses of the 1983 films, these contemporary Carmens are vibrant, proud, self-confident women who celebrate life, ethnicity, and community.

ROBERT TOWNSEND'S *CARMEN: A HIP HOPERA* (2001)

Robert Townsend's *Carmen: A Hip Hopera*, produced for MTV, launched the career of a new star, the singer Beyoncé, in the role of Carmen, an aspiring actress (Figure 3.9). Townsend substitutes original hip-hop music for Bizet's original score, hip-hop being the popular acoustic marker of black urban America at the start of the millennium. In Bizet's opera, Zuniga, José's lieutenant, has only a minor role, but in *Carmen: A Hip Hopera* Townsend gives a major part to the police Lieutenant Miller (played by Mos Def),

FIGURE 3.9   Clip of Beyoncé Knowles in *Carmen: A Hip Hopera* by Robert Towsend (USA, 2001).

a cop on the take who shakes down drug dealers. Because Sergeant Hill (Bizet's José, played by Mekhi Pfifer) could expose his transgressions, Miller arranges to have Hill ousted from the police department.

Hill and Carmen leave Philadelphia for Los Angeles in the hope that Carmen can pursue an acting career. But neither Carmen nor Hill will succeed in finding work. When Carmen goes to hear the popular rapper Blaze, the Escamillo of Bizet's opera, Hill follows Carmen to the theater in an attempt to win her back, but Hill has also been followed to the theater by Miller. In Townsend's version, it is the rogue policeman Miller who kills Carmen by shooting her in the back while she and Hill are arguing. Hill pursues Miller on the flies of the theater, they fight, and Miller falls onto the stage. According to a reporter on the scene, Hill is arrested for having committed a crime of passion. In Townsend's film, Carmen is killed by a rogue policeman and the Hill-José character is falsely accused. Black pride and community spirit are expressed by the rap musical rhythm that provide the film's vocal narrative. *Carmen: A Hip Hopera* starts and ends with an extra-diegetic female narrator who tells the story, a story representing aspects of the social difficulties encountered by many African Americans at the dawn of the new century, thereby giving it an historical as well as a mythical dimension.

JOSEPH GAÏ RAMAKA'S *KARMEN GEÏ* (2001)

Music, the rhythmic beat of drums, and flashes of color from the women's *boubou* dresses explode on the screen even before the title *Karmen Geï* appears. The film starts with Karmen (played by Djeïnaba Diop Gaï) dancing a *Sabar*, a popular Senegalese dance. The landscapes, languages, gestures, and clothing lend the film a kind of general African sensibility, but for (film scholar) Françoise Pfaff, it is the singing, the painted faces of those impersonating the dead, the reddish-yellow hue of the island of Gorée, and the glittering of the sea that designate Ramaka's film as distinctly Senegalese (Figure 3.10).[16]

The bullfighting metaphor of the opera appears at the very opening of the film, with the dance of the *Sabar* set in a circular courtyard backed by the arched doors of one of the infamous prisons of Gorée, from which African slaves were shipped to the New World. Sitting on a chair, dressed entirely in black, legs apart, ready to pounce, Karmen, as

FIGURE 3.10   Clip of *Karmen Geï* by Joseph Gaï Ramaka (France/Canada/Senegal, 2001).

she is first glimpsed onscreen, seems to masquerade as a bull. Ramaka's arena is a dance area on a sand-covered ground, a scene of erotic seduction, where Carmen's *Sabar* beguiles the female prison warden, Angélique (played by Stéphanie Biddle), who will make Karmen's escape from prison possible.

In addition to its references to Bizet's opera, Ramaka's film also follows the plot of Mérimée's novella by portraying Karmen as the leader of a band of smugglers. But Ramaka adds a number of characters to Mérimée's plot: Angélique, with whom Karmen has a lesbian liaison, and Karmen's mother, Ma Penda (Dienaba Niang). Ramaka also introduces some of Karmen's former lovers, Massigi (played by El Hadj Ndiaye, a well-known Senegalese pop star) and Old Samba (Thierno Ndiaye Doss). These added characters allow Karmen to express a gamut of feelings, giving new depth to her personality. We watch her heartbroken when she hides in church at Angélique's funeral. Although she is portrayed as a strong woman, she turns to Massigi when in need of support. She has deeply emotional ties with Samba, with whom she reminisces.

Ramaka gives prominence to music and dance and includes a range of Senegalese social activities, which morph the French Carmen into the Senegalese Karmen. The mix of Wolof and French on the soundtrack reference Senegal's past as a French colony. The postcolonial scholar Anjali Prabhu finds that "the film brilliantly creates an Africa-oriented spectator who is actually seduced into questioning the authority of the European myth against the film's definitive adherence to it."[17] And the film scholar Lindiwe Dovey observes: "*Karmen Geï* not only provides a strikingly distinct representation of the story but also succeeds in strategically revitalizing the myth at its source by adapting to the anxieties of Mérimée's and Bizet's versions while simultaneously radically revising them from a self-confident and critical African point of view."[18]

The turn of the twenty-first century was a time of political fervor in Senegal. It saw the end of the nineteen-year reign of President Abdou Diouf, the election of opposition leader Abdoulaye Wade, and the ratification a new constitution. In a lengthy interview with Michael Martin, Ramaka declared, "A collective struggle has meaning only for the extent that it is rooted in each individual consciousness. My concerns are not as a filmmaker, but rather as a citizen who happens to be a filmmaker and who believes that he has the means to act as a citizen with what he knows best." He reiterates his position a little later in the interview, "I am not a filmmaker *engagé*. I am an ordinary citizen *engagé*. I want the rank-and-file, the policemen, filmmaker, administrator, and judge to be *engagé* as self-conscious citizens."[19] In Ramaka's film, Karmen is the poster woman for such engagement, making political statements and acting as someone free from any kind of social constraint, including conventional sexual relationships.

When Karmen learns through the Tarot cards of her imminent death, she sees masked figures of the past. She is killed in the fly of a theater, while onstage a well-known Senegalese singer chants about her life. In death, Karmen becomes, through the singer's narrative, a mythic figure that incarnates present-day Senegalese culture against the backdrop of its historical past.

DIMPHO DI KOPANE'S *U-CARMEN* (2005)

Produced by the South African theater company Dimpho Di Kopane, *U-Carmen* is a film shot on location in the South African shantytown of Khayelitsha (Figure 3.11). In

FIGURE 3.11   Clip of film *U-Carmen* E-khayelitsha by the Dimpho Di Kopane theater (South Africa, 2005).

GEORGES BIZET'S *CARMEN*

the film, Dimpho Di Kopane conveys a sense of contemporary South African identity by having cast members speak and sing the libretto of Bizet's opera in Xhosa, a Bantu language with distinctive consonant clicks. The audible result is astonishing. In *U-Carmen*, Carmen works in a cigarette factory and José is a sergeant in the local police force.

In an interview, the film's director Mark Dornford-May explained that for him, Carmen is not a figure known primarily for what she does to men. Rather, she is whatever men make her become.[20] In a startling departure from other versions, Carmen falls to the ground after having been hit by the police captain, who has come for sex as payment for not having arrested her earlier. The role of Carmen is played by the singer Pauline Malefane, who helped translate the libretto into Xhosa. For Malefane, Carmen is simply a woman who wants to live life to the fullest. She perceives Carmen as somewhat selfish, a person who does not care what others think of her. But she also understands her to be fragile, despite appearing strong on the outside.

Although it uses Bizet's score, *U-Carmen* is not a filmed version of Bizet's opera; the score is not always exactly followed and Bizet's music is often interrupted by the singing and dancing of the people of the shantytown. These moments add local color and unexpected vibrancy to the strictly operatic staging of *Carmen*. The toreador is an acclaimed opera singer, a cousin of Carmen, who comes back home to retire and is briefly shown on television in his stage role as Escamillo. At the end of the film, José kills Carmen outside the theater where the townspeople welcome back the famous baritone. We learn that José is in the police force because his mother suspected that he killed his brother in a fit of anger and she banned him from home. As the camera moves away for a closing aerial shot, the crime scene is visibly marked outside the theater, where the toreador's song unites the shantytown's community. The social bond between women is highlighted at the end when, as members of the chorus, Carmen's women friends wear the same dress as Carmen when she is killed. Here we are presented with a visual understanding that all women may face Carmen's fate.

* * *

In contrast to many earlier cinematic renditions, these films of the new millennium seem less fascinated by the "*femme fatale.*" Except for the stunningly beautiful Beyoncé of Townsend's hip-hop Carmen, neither Karmen nor the Carmen of the Dimpho Di Kopane theater company is a Hollywood type of beauty. They are women with distinctive physical appearances and strong, self-affirming personalities. All three films seem less focused on the love story per se than on the social context within which the love story takes place. They transmit a political vision by showing the social issues facing the protagonists, referencing historical events, recording indigenous music, or representing community traditions. In these way, these all-black-cast Carmens expand the legacy of Preminger's *Carmen Jones*, and one could add Saura's and Rosi's Carmens among the films that celebrate specific communities and traditions. These directors use the sound track to transmit examples of ethnic music in addition to the images of indigenous people, their habitats, or folkoric dance and art forms. Like *la musica e le parole* in opera, or an extra-diegetic commentary in a literary text, the visual narrative and the soundtrack in film often tell distinctive stories. Occasionally, these dual paths of expression in their dialogical exchange provide the listener, the reader, and the spectator with an opening for a different understanding of the work. In their distinctive renditions of the Carmen story, films provide records of the changing interests of audiences across generations and geographies. They call attention to elements of Bizet's opera and Mérimée's novella that had earlier been less immediately apparent, and they offer, sometimes retrospectively, new perspectives on our canonic understandings of the Carmen story.

CONCLUSION

SITES OF SEDUCTION

"To venture into the field of Carmenology," writes Adrian Rifkin, "is to acquire for oneself a position in the terrain of the truly banal."[1] Given the popularity of Carmen, any discourse on it—whether a remake of the story or a critical exercise like the one in this book—partakes of the *déjà vu (already seen)*, the *déjà entendu* (already heard), or *déjà lu* (already read), and thereby defies any claim to originality. But beyond its ironic charge, Rifkin's pithy comment calls attention to the making of banality—*banal* deriving from the Latin *bannum*, meaning a ban, a decree, or a proclamation. Rifkin's terse remark reminds us that any interpretation—especially any reading of such a popular story as Carmen—requires that we position ourselves in relation to "the truly banal": not simply in relation to that

Georges Bizet's Carmen. Nelly Furman, Oxford University Press (2020). © Oxford University Press.
DOI: 10.1093/oso/9780190059149.001.0001

which may be commonplace, but more pertinently to that which *decrees* what is conventional. In other words, the law, the "ban," the assumptions according to which we decide what is cliché and what is not.

The persistence of the Carmen myth through time and across media, cultures, and continents indicates that its plot can accommodate many variations in the development of its narrative. The skeleton story of Carmen—she no longer loves him, he kills her—is no more than a hackneyed, stereotypical crime-of-passion story. However, this timeworn plot is precisely what makes the story an alluring challenge for creative talents. For while the plot may be commonplace, it is the treatment of a cliché that turns banality into art. If banality resides in the plot, artistry expresses itself in the telling of the plot. Linda Hutcheon and Siobhan O'Flynn speak of the "not so subtle denigration of adaptation in our (late-Romantic, capitalist) culture that still tends to value 'the original,' despite the ubiquity and longevity of adaptation as a mode of retelling our favorite stories."[2] There is indeed a long-held tradition in Western thought of regarding "originality" as the acme of artistic creation. The issue, then, is where one locates the notion of originality. Does originality reside in the story itself or in the manner in which the story is being presented? Myths, in contrast, acquire their status not for relying on an original or originating source, but rather for their noticeable and frequent presence as cultural objects or events over time. Through multiple iterations and duplications, stories are transformed into myths. It is then that the idea of originality is displaced from the plot itself into its treatments and transfigurations.

The popularity of the Carmen story is precisely the essence of its mythical dimension.

The first act of Bizet's opera sets the normative romantic background: Micaëla is the expected bride to be, children are seen imitating soldiers, and soldiers mill around, engaging in flirting banter with female passersby. Marriage and children form the background of the happy social order depicted in the opening scene. It is this patriarchal system of sanctified sexual relations that Carmen's and José's liaison puts into question.

In his study *Love as Passion. The Codification of Intimacy*, the German sociologist Niklas Luhmann points out that in much of Europe until the end of the eighteenth century, the upper classes formed the state's support structure and marriages were arranged to maintain class status. With the erosion of the power of the upper classes, marital relations no longer served this purpose, and this in turn allowed the option of individual choice in marriage:

> By the eighteenth century families from the upper social strata had already lost their significance as "supporters of the state." Social-structural reasons for controls on marriage had thus ceased to exist, and what was there to prevent society from making the switch from arranged marriages to marriages of the heart?[3]

Luhmann points out that before "marriages of the heart" became the norm, "passion" had the purpose of warding off attempts by family or society by emphasizing the pathological lack of responsibility for one's own feelings and actions. Things start to change at the end of the eighteenth century, when passion loses its reference as a pathology and becomes testimony of one's freedom to love and neither it nor its consequences needed to be justified. This is first illustrated in French literature by the novel of the Abbé Prévost, *Histoire du chevalier Des Grieux et de Manon Lescaut* (1731), that will be the source of operas by Jules Massenet (*Manon*, 1882) and Giacomo Puccini (*Manon Lescaut*, 1892). As evidenced by Bizet, Massenet, and Puccini, nineteenth-century operas celebrate passionate love as an astonishing event, an overwhelming emotion occurring often at first sight. With marriages of the heart, love became the driving concept of intimacy and intrinsically linked with sexuality. In Luhmann's view, love is "nothing other than the ideal expression and systematization of the sexual drive."[4] Social norms trickle down from the upper classes, and José's transition of love objects from Micaëla, the expected spouse in an arranged marriage, to Carmen, the object of his personal attraction, reflects this change in societal view of passion as an accepted form of attraction.

In the opera, Carmen's murder is presented as a crime of passion. In Mérimée's novella it is a crime motivated by jealousy, but also supported by misogyny, and substantiated by racism. Crimes of passion, like racist hate crimes, are evidence of the unacknowledged value and unexamined personal capital represented by male hegemony in some patriarchal societies, and by whiteness in some social milieux and geographical spaces. In this respect, Carmen's murder speaks powerfully to women and men in their personal relationships to others, in their individual support of, or dissent from, societal values. As several film adaptations have made clear, societal values are the focus of films presenting national and ethnic communities.

In Latin, *sacrificium* (sacrifice) is a combination of *sacer* (sacred) and *facere* (to make). Sacrifice and the sacred share an etymological root and are interdependent. Is one sacrificed because one is sacred, or is one sacred because one is sacrificed? José's final words are significant in this regard: "You can arrest me. I killed her, my adored Carmen." Carmen, the woman he worships, is an idol and thus supposedly deserving of sacrifice as a gesture of adulation. A form of sacrifice, sacrifice of self or of the Other, is at the center of the dynamics of seduction. From the Latin *seducer*, seduction is the action of leading one astray, or, in its passive form, of being led astray. Leading or being led astray supposes that there is a standard of behavior being violated. The word thus carries a negative value that applies to both the seducer and the one seduced. In this context, Carmen and José are both responsible for violating social norms of conduct. Both bear responsibility for their individual actions and also for their straying. In this optic, it is therefore impossible to characterize either José or Carmen as innocent victims.

The literary critic Jean Starobinski suggests that the figures of seducer and seductress, "created by mythic imagination, may date from the earliest consciousness of lying. They seem to have been invented as soon as the distinction became established between obedience and disobedience, between the good path and erring, and the alternative between living and perishing."[5] No wonder language plays a major role in both Mérimée's novella and Bizet's opera.

For the philosopher Jean Baudrillard, seduction appears as a liability in the bourgeois economy of production, for seduction is a game, an artificial effect, a ritualized form of secretive interaction, whereas production relies on visible, material evidence.[6] The issue of work and production appears in the very first act of the opera, when Carmen's action stops work in the tobacco factory, and again in the second, when the smugglers ask the women to play their role by flirting with the customs agents.[7]

Flirting is the principal mode of communication, the strategic skill in the game of seduction, and Carmen, who exudes charm, physical sensuality, and verbal virtuosity, is a master when it comes to the art of flirtation. To quote from psychoanalyst Adam Phillips,

> The generosity of flirtation is in its implicit wish to sustain the life of desire; and often by blurring, or putting into question the boundary been sex and sexualization. Flirting creates the uncertainty it is also trying to control; and so can make us wonder which ways of knowing or being known, sustain our interest, our excitement, in other people.[8]

In this light, Carmen is a flirt because she wants to be desiring and also to be desired. With respect to this, to continue with Phillips, "It is one of the advantages of flirtation that it can protect us from idolatry—and its opposite—while acknowledging the draw of such grand absolutes. Flirting, in other words, is often an unconscious form of skepticism."[9]

The common contention that the relationship between José and Carmen (or Carmen and José) can be described as one of victim and victimizer may blur the fact that each of them shares the same need and emotional demand: a desire to love and to be loved. Most stories represented on stage, on screen, and in literature present love as an unquestioned, accepted fact. *Carmen*, however, distinguishes itself precisely because it puts love itself into question. While not always acknowledged, love, as the principal unresolved issue between the two protagonists, is surely another element that has sustained Carmen's immense popularity. What is love? Is it Carmen's pursuit of objects of desire, or is it José's intense and binding attachment? In Bizet's opera, Carmen's embrace of love as a transitory moment offers a palliative to the exclusive and permanent adoration cherished by José.

In Western cultures, love is imbued with the romantic notion of similarity of emotion, emblematized in a fusing or coming together of two individual beings. This representation of love, and its occasional failure, forms the basis of much of Western literature and art. In his analysis of the discourse of love, Barthes writes that "through a perversion truly love's own, it is love that one loves, not its object of affection."[10] James Joyce expressed a similar thought in *Ulysses*: "Love loves to love love."[11] Is love itself, rather than the lover, the object of attraction? If so, then one could also suggest that José's attachment is a function of his desire for love, and not necessarily for Carmen per se. As for Carmen, as we saw earlier, it is desire itself, and not necessarily a specific lover, that is her object of interest. The echoing effect of the word *love*, in Barthes's and Joyce's aphorisms, signals a playful reference to the myth of Narcissus and Echo, for here it is narcissism rather than altruism that triggers the heartbeat of love. While Western art most often presents an idealized and unquestioned notion of love, Bizet's *Carmen* shatters that notion by revealing the egoism at its very core.

Like all aspects of human life, love is always conceived and understood through the lens of one's social culture. In the past, arranged marriages assured the continued status and power of the elites through controlled reproduction, which also assured and defined the roles of the sexes not only within marriage but in society at large. Now that love rather than social status has more widely become the principal motivator in coupledom, the place and function of men and women within the intimate relationship has also shifted. Luhmann sees it this way:

> The differences between the sexes—which were emphasized in all love codes in the past, and around which asymmetries were constructed and enhanced—are toned down. Considering that this difference used to be an even more important criterion for marriage than money, the question today is what to do with the remains of a difference that cannot be legitimated?[12]

The modernity of Bizet's opera may reside precisely in the erosion of gender differences in the personalities of Carmen and José, thus opening the possibility of recognizing relationships and marriage between individuals independently from their gender.

In addition to the themes of love and sexuality that are continually revisited, issues of identity, alterity, difference, and individuation have generated considerable interest in recent Western culture. Yet crucially, in this ideological context, however attractive the otherness of the Other may be, that otherness remains beyond anyone's grasp. However close, akin, or beloved another might be, he or she is not me, and I am not him or her. I can share, enjoy, commiserate, or sympathize with another's beautiful or miserable moments, but I cannot fully identify with him or her—that is to say, I cannot be in subjective empathy. To this extent, the other remains an enigma that always recedes to new depths at our attempts to fully understand that person. For the philosopher Emmanuel Levinas, "relation with the other is not an idyllic and harmonic relation of communion nor some sympathy whereby we recognize the other as similar to us, but still outside of us; the relation with the other is a relation with a mystery."[13] Love, in this view, cannot be conceived as a fusional relationship. Rather, it can only be understood as a reciprocal exchange: not as a duet but as a dialogue, a constant give-and-take. In the age of the other, the story of Carmen and José claims a place at center stage.

Today, when traditional gender norms and behaviors are being challenged, Bizet's instantly recognized score is often used to signal a moment of self-affirmation, or conditions of being that continue to defy social norms and expectations. In a film of 2014 entitled *Dear White People*, directed by Justin Simien, the music of the Habanera underscores the moment when a young African American male college student feels ready to abandon his position on the campus newspaper to follow his own calling. In a play of 2015 by Simon Stephens entitled *Carmen Disruption*, Carmen is a young male prostitute, José is a female cab driver, Micaëla is a teenage girl, and Escamillo a futures trader. In Detroit, on June 17, 2016, Opera MODO staged *Carmen* inside a women's prison. The role of Carmen was performed by a countertenor, playing a transgender woman. At the 2017 Summer Festival of Aix-en-Provence, director Dimitri Tcherniakov staged the opera in a clinic to help the sexually repressed José and Carmen survive death, the stabbing scene being a psychodrama meant to help José overcome his inhibitions. For the 2018 program of the London Royal Opera House at Covent Garden, Barrie Kosky presented a modernized *Carmen* stripped of Spanish iconography where it is she who kills José. For new generations, Bizet's opera may yet serve as a vehicle for the affirmation of personal agency, the appeal of unexpected emotions, and the complexities of gender and sexuality.

The many themes arising in Bizet's opera and Mérimée's novella—misogyny, racism, claims to scientific authority, social needs, economic productivity, cultural identity, personal desire, and the many faces of love—present a multitude of contested sites as sources of inspiration for artists in all media. Like all myths, the Carmen myth is a story that speaks to communities and individuals by addressing their fears, acknowledging their conflicts, noting their struggles, and expressing their losses. The stories they tell may appear familiar, common, and even humdrum to some. "Banality," in Barthes's words, "is a discourse without a body."[14] When interpreted, given expressivity, and a viewpoint, the banality of plot is transformed into art. In the future, Carmen's self-affirming voice and José's sense of loss will be shown anew, performed by other artists, paced by different conductors, and imagined by new film directors, and each new production will reflect the joys and anxieties of individuals within a community at a given time. That is, after all, the magic of art.

SOURCES FOR FURTHER READING, LISTENING, AND VIEWING

Since Jean Roy's monumental biography of Bizet from 1983 (Editions du Seuil), two new voluminous biographies have been published in France: *Georges Bizet* by Rémy Stricker (Gallimard, 1999), and *Bizet* by Hervé Lacombe (Fayard, 2000). In English, the best biographical sources are Cynthia Klohr's recent translation from German of Christoph Schwandt's *Georges Bizet* (Scarecrow Press, 2013) and Hugh Macdonald's *Bizet* (Oxford University Press, 2014). An invaluable source on Bizet's opera that intersects with this study on several points while also pursuing different approaches and aims is Susan McClary's *Georges Bizet: Carmen* (Cambridge University Press, 1992). Extensions of some of this book's discussions into other operatic repertoires include *Opera through Other Eyes*, edited by David J. Levin (Stanford University Press, 1993), in which a number of prominent cultural theorists and critics seek to displace traditional approaches to 'hearing and reading opera; and Michel Poizat's *The Angel's Cry: Beyond the Pleasure Principle in Opera* (Cornell University Press, 1992), which draws on psychoanalytic theory to understand voice in the context of emotion and gender.

The filmography available in *Carmen on Film: A Cultural History*, edited by Phil Powrie, Bruce Babington, Ann Davies, and Chris Perriam, is invaluable for cinematic productions through 2004 and *Carmen: From Silent Film to MTV*, a compilation of essays edited by Chris Perriam and Ann Davies. These two volumes should now be augmented by films produced since then: the Senegalese *Karmen Geï* and *U-Carmen* from South Africa, *Carmen from Kawachi* (1966) directed by Seijun Suzuki and shown at Lincoln Center in 2016, as well as the notable eighty-minute stage hit by Peter Brook, *La Tragédie de Carmen* (1983), available on film.

NOTES

INTRODUCTION

1   Margaret Croyden, *Conversations with Peter Brook 1970–2000* (New York: Faber and Faber, 2003), 189.

2   Modeste Tchaikovsky, *The Life & Letters of Peter Ilich Tchaikovsky*. Edited from the Russian with an introduction by Rosa Newmarch (New York: Haskell House Publishers Ltd, 1970), Vol. 1, 382.

3   Arrangements using Bizet's score have inspired many ballets, and two have become classics in the world of dance. The *Carmen Suite* in the repertoire of the Bolshoi Ballet, choreographed by Alberto Alonso with a musical arrangement by Rodion Shchedrin, featured some of the Bolshoi's greatest ballerinas since 1967, Svetlana Zakharova and Maya Plisetskaya. And Roland Petit created a *Carmen* ballet in 1949, with music arranged by Tommy Desserre, which was revived in 1980 with Zizi Jeanmaire and Mikhail Baryshnikov in the title roles.

4   On Broadway, Bizet's score accompanies the demure librarian of *The Music Man* when she engages in a mock seduction scene. The skaters were East German Katarina Witt and American Debi Thomas. Katarina Witt won the Gold Medal for her performance and went on to star in an 86-minute dance film based on Bizet's opera, *Carmen on Ice*. The film won an Emmy Award for outstanding Performance in Classical Music/Dance Programing in 1990.

5   Prosper Mérimée, letter to Madame de Montijo, May 16, 1845, in his *Correspondance générale* (Paris: le Divan, 1941–1947), Vol. 4, 294.

6   Claude Lévi-Strauss, *Structural Anthropology*, trans. Claire Jacobson and Brooke Grundfest Schoepf (New York and London: Basic Books, 1963), 218.

7   Susan McClary, "Structures of Identity and Difference in Bizet's *Carmen*," in *The Work of Opera, Genre, Nationhood, and Sexual Difference*, ed. Richard Dellamora and Daniel Fischlin (New York: Columbia University Press, 1997), 128.

8 Thomas Mann, *The Magic Mountain*, trans. Jon E. Woods (New York: Vintage, 1996), 602.

9 Léon Poliakov, *Le mythe aryen. Essai sur les sources du racisme et des nationalismes* (Paris: Editions Complexe, 1987), 214.

10 Roger Callois, *Le mythe et l'homme* (Paris: Gallimard, 1938), 13.

11 Julia Kristeva, *Strangers to Ourselves*, trans. Leon S. Roudiez (New York: Columbia University Press, 1991), 3.

12 Adam Phillips, "Against Self-Criticism," *London Review of Books*, March 5, 2015, 13.

13 Callois, *Le mythe et l'homme*, 17.

CHAPTER 1

1 Friedrich Nietzsche, *The Case of Wagner*, in *The Anti-Christ, Ecce Homo, Twilight of the Idols, and Other Writings*, ed. Aaron Ridley and Judith Norman, trans. Judith Norman (Cambridge: Cambridge University Press, 2005), 236 (emphasis in original).

2 Mario Praz, *The Romantic Agony*, 2nd ed., trans. Angus Davidson (Oxford: Oxford University Press, 1970), 207.

3 Michel Leiris, *Manhood: A Journey from Childhood into the Fierce Order of Virility*, trans. Richard Howard (New York: Grossman, 1963), 54.

4 Phil Powrie, Bruce Babington, Ann Davies, and Chris Perriam, *Carmen on Film: A Cultural History* (Bloomington and Indianapolis: Indiana University Press, 2007), 19 (emphasis in original).

5 Michel Rabaud, "Carmen: A Tragedy of Love, Sun, and Death," *English National Opera Guide* 13 (1982): 39.

6 Catherine Clément, *Opera, or the Undoing of Women* (Minneapolis: University of Minnesota Press, 1988), 48 and 53.

7 See Susan McClary, *Georges Bizet: Carmen* (Cambridge: Cambridge University Press, 1992), 123.

8 Henry Malherbe, *Carmen* (Paris: Editions Albin Michel, 1951), 305.

9 Theodor W. Adorno, "Fantasia sopra Carmen," in his *Quasi una fantasia: Essays on Modern Music*, trans. Rodney Livingstone (London and New York: Verso, 1992), 62–63.

10 *Et songe en combattant / Qu'un oeil noir te regarde /et que l'amour t'attend.*

11 Dominique Maingueneau, *Carmen: Les Racines d'un mythe* (Paris: Editions du Sorbier, 1984), 80.

12 Roland Barthes, *Sur Racine* (Paris: Editions du Seuil, 1963), 26.

13 Philippe-Joseph Salazar, *Idéologies de l'opéra* (Paris: Presses Universitaires de France, 1980), 139–140.

14 Salazar, *Idéologies*, 178–187.

15 Catherine Clément and Julia Kristeva, *Le Féminin et le sacré* (Paris: Editions Stock, 1998), 231.

16 Maingueneau, *Carmen: Les Racines d'un mythe*, 28.

17 Hélène Cixous and Catherine Clément, *The Newly Born Woman* (Minneapolis: University of Minnesota Press, 1986), 86.

18 Roland Barthes, *Fragments d'un discours amoureux* (Paris: Editions du Seuil, 1977), 20.

19 Nietzsche, *Case of Wagner*, 236 (emphasis in original).

20 *L'amour est enfant de Bohême, Il n'a jamais, jamais connu de loi. . . . Tu crois le tenir, il t'évite; Tu crois l'éviter, il te tient.*

21 Adorno, "Fantasie sopra Carmen," 63.

22 On these two modes of love, see Evelyn Gould, *The Fate of Carmen* (Baltimore and London: Johns Hopkins University Press, 1996), 108–114.

23 *Ne crains rien, ma mère, ton fils t'obéira, fera ce que tu lui dis, j'aime Micaëla, je la prendrai pour femme.*

24 *Ainsi, le salut de mon âme je l'aurai perdu pour que toi—pour que tu t'en ailles, infâme, entre ses bras rire de moi!*

25 René Girard, *La violence et le sacré* (Paris: Editions Grasset, 1972), 145–146.

26 Compare this passage from Mérimée's text: "Then I heard more officers saying a number of things to her that made the colour mount on my cheeks. I could no hear her replies. It was that day, I think, that I fell in love with her in earnest" (Prosper Mérimée, *Carmen and Other Stories*, trans. Nicholas Jotcham [Oxford and New York: Oxford University Press, 1989], 28).

27 Barthes, *Fragments*, 80.

28 Luce Irigaray, *This Sex Which Is Not One*, trans. Catherine Porter (Ithaca, NY: Cornell University Press, 1985), 193.

29 David Wills, "Carmen: Sound/Effect," *Cinema Journal* 25, no. 4 (summer 1986): 36.

30 Mary Ann Doane, *Femmes Fatales: Feminism, Film Theory, Psychoanalysis* (New York and London: Routledge, 1991), 2.

31 *Tu demandes l'impossible, Carmen jamais n'a menti, Son âme reste inflexible. Entre elle et toi, c'est fini.*

32 Barthes, *Fragments*, 175–183.

33 Paul Landormy, *Bizet* (Paris: Gallimard, 1950), 185; McClary, "Structures of Identity and Difference in Bizet's *Carmen*," 125.

34 *Non tu ne m'aimes pas! Non! car si tu m'aimais, Là-bas, là-bas tu me suivrais.*

35 *Carmen, il est temps encore, O ma Carmen, laisse-moi te sauver, toi que j'adore, Et me sauver avec toi!*

36 *Tu crois le tenir, il t'évite. Tu veux l'éviter, il te tient.*

37 Michel Cardoze, *Georges Bizet* (Paris: Mazarine Musique, 1982), 50.

38 *Et vieux chrétien. Don José Lizzarabengoa, c'est mon nom.*

39 She does so in Mérimée, *Carmen and Other Stories*, 30.

40 Claude Lévi-Strauss, *The Savage Mind* (Chicago: University of Chicago Press, 1966), 17.

41 Lévi-Strauss, *Savage Mind*, 17.

42 For further discussion of the functions of the bullfighting arenas see the discussion of Francesco Rosi's film in chapter 3.

43 Winton Dean, *Georges Bizet: His Life and Work* (London: J. M. Dent, 1965), 224.

44 Teresa Berganza, "Ma Carmen," *L'Avant-Scène*, March 26, 1980, 117.

45 *Mais quant à être aimé de moi pour le moment, il ne faut pas y penser.*

46 On this issue, see Shoshana Felman, *The Literary Speech Act: Don Juan with J. L. Austin, or Seduction in Two Languages*, trans. Catherine Porter (Ithaca, NY: Cornell University Press, 1983), 11.

47 *Je paie mes dettes c'est notre loi à nous autres bohémiennes, je paie mes dettes, je paie mes dettes.*

48 In a recent biography of Bizet, Rémy Stricker calls Carmen "a female Don Juan"; see Rémy Stricker, *Georges Bizet (1838–1875)* (Paris: Gallimard, 1999), 88.

49 Louis Viardot, *Etudes sur l'histoire des institutions, de la littérature, du théâtre et des beaux-arts en Espagne* (Paris: Paulin, 1835).

50 Theodor Adorno, "Bourgeois Opera," trans. David J. Levin, in *Opera through Other Eyes*, ed. Levin (Stanford, CA: Stanford University Press, 1993), 33–36.

51 McClary, *Georges Bizet: Carmen*, 67.

52 Denis de Rougemont, *L'Amour et l'Occident* (Paris: Librairie Plon, 1939), 269 and 260–261.

53 For a detailed analysis of the relation between Mérimée's novella and Bizet's opera, see Christine Rodriguez, *Les Passions du récit à l'opéra. Rhétorique de la transposition dans Carmen, Mireille, Manon* (Paris: Classiques Garnier, 2009), 3.

54 McClary, *Georges Bizet: Carmen*, 17.

55 Mina Curtiss, *Bizet and His World* (New York: Alfred A. Knopf, 1958), 351.

56 Cardoze, *Georges Bizet*, 50.

57 Jean Roy, *Bizet* (Paris: Editions du Seuil, 1983), 7.

58 Cardoze, *Georges Bizet*, 51.

59 See Mérimée, *Carmen*, 13.

60 For a detailed consideration of this issue in the opera, see McClary, *Georges Bizet: Carmen*, 51–58; and more generally, Ralph P. Locke, *Musical Exoticism: Images and Reflections* (Cambridge: Cambridge University Press, 2009), 169–174.

61 Malherbe, *Carmen*, 190–191.

62 Mérimée, *Correspondance générale* (Paris: Le Divan, 1941–1947), Vol. 4, 294.

63 Cardoze, *Georges Bizet*, 149–150.

64 Stricker, *Georges Bizet 1838–1875*, 195.

65 Cathy Caruth, "Introduction," *American Imago: Studies in Psychoanalysis and Culture* 48 (1991): 7.

66 Gertrud Koch, "The Angel of Forgetfulness and the Black Box of Facticity: Trauma and Memory in Claude Lanzmann's Film *Shoah*," *History and Memory* 3 (1991): 131.

67 Georges Bizet and Claude Glayman, *Lettres 1850–1875* (Paris: Calmann-Lévi, 1989), 275–276.

68 Carl Dahlhaus, *Realism in Nineetenth-Century Music*, trans. Mary Whittall (Cambridge: Cambridge University Press, 1985), 89 and 91–92.

69 Stricker, *Georges Bizet,* 168

CHAPTER 2

1 Mérimée, *Carmen and Other Stories*, 1–53. Chapter 4 appears in the Appendix, pp. 333–339. Here throughout this chapter, page references to the novella are indicated in parentheses.

2 See George M. Fredrickson, *Racism: A Short History* (Princeton, NJ: Princeton University Press, 2002).

3 Changing a letter in a word to change its meaning is a popular word game in France called "une contre-pettrie," similar to an English spoonerism.

4 For a general introduction to the history of the people of Roma, see Lou Charmon-Deutsch's book, *The Spanish Gypsy: The History of a European Obsession* (University Park: Pennsylvania State University Press, 2004).

5 Heinrich Moritz Gottlieb Grellmann, *Historischer Versuch über die Zigeuner* (Göttingen: Johann Christian Dieterich, 1787).

6 Poliakov, *Le mythe aryen*, 214.

7 George Henry Borrow, *The Zincali: An Account of the Gypsies of Spain*. New impression. [Des Moines, Iowa]: LBS Archival Products, 1988.

8 Judith Okely, *The Traveller-Gypsies* (Cambridge: Cambridge University Press, 1983), 8.

9 Poliakov, *Le mythe aryen*, 177–214.

10 Okely, *Traveler-Gypsies*, 9–10.

11 Benedict Anderson, *Imagined Communities* (London and New York: Verso, 1991), 149–150 (emphasis in original).

12 André Billy, *Mérimée* (Paris: Flammarion, 1959), 153.

13 Mérimée, *Correspondance générale*, Vol. 4, 389.

14 Daniel Sibony, *Ecrits sur le racisme* (Paris: Christian Bourgois Editeur, 1988), 16.

15 Alan William Raitt, *Prosper Mérimée* (New York: Scribner, 1970), 193.

16 Mérimée, *Correspondance générale*, Vol. 4, 294.

17 Jean Borie, *Mythologies de l'hérédité au XIXe siècle* (Paris: Editions Galilée, 1981), 14.

18 Borie, *Mythologies*, 101–102.

19 Gould, *The Fate of Carmen* (Baltimore and London: Johns Hopkins University Press, 1996), 18–59. See also Susan McClary, *Georges Bizet: Carmen* (Cambridge: Cambridge University Press, 1991), 35–43.

20 Honoré de Balzac, "A Prince of Bohemia" (1840), in *The Novels of Honoré de Balzac*, trans. Janet Minot Sedgwick (Philadelphia: George Barrie, 1896), 364–366.

21 Charnon-Deutsch, *The Spanish Gypsy: The History of a European Obsession* (University Park: Pennsylvania State University Press, 2004), 11.

CHAPTER 3

1 *Carmen. From Silent Film to MTV*, ed. Chris Perriam and Ann Davies (Amesterdam and New York: Rodopi, 2005). Phil Powrie, Bruce Babington, Ann Davies, and Chris Perriam, *Carmen on Film. A Cultural History* (Bloomington and Indianapolis: Indiana Univerity Press, 2007).

2 Powrie, Babington, Davies, and Perriam, *Carmen on Film*, 32.

3 *Non, tu ne m'aimes pas! Non, car si tu m'aimais, là-bas, là-bas, tu me suivrais. Sur ton cheval tu me prendrais, et comme un brave à travers la campagne, en croupe, tu m'emporterais* (Act II, Scene 3).

4 Laura Mulvey, *Visual and Other Pleasures* (Bloomington and Indianapolis: Indiana University Press, 1989), 19.

5 Mulvey, *Visual and Other Pleasures*, 18.

6 Quoted in Donald Bogle, *Dorothy Dandridge: A Biography* (New York: Amistad, 1997), 277.

7 A noteworthy exeption was famed contralto Marian Anderson, who enthralled concertgoers but integrated New York's Metropolitan Opera only in 1955, a year after Preminger's *Carmen Jones*.

8 Michel Mardore, "Toutes les femme s'appellent Carmen," *Le Nouvel Observateur*, August 19, 1983.

9 Perriam and Davies, *Carmen*, 2.

10 Powrie, Babington, Davies, and Perriam, *Carmen on Film*, 30.

11 Roland Barthes, *Roland Barthes par Roland Barthes* (Paris: Seuil, 1975), 48–49.

12 Jeremy Tambling, *Opera, Ideology, and Film* (New York: St. Martin's Press, 1987), 36–37.

13 H. Marshall Leicester, "Discourse and the Film Text: Four Readings of Carmen," *Cambridge Opera Journal* 6 (1994): 268–269.

14 Leicester, "Discourse," 269.

15 For more on the film, see Phil Powrie, "Jean-Luc's Women (Godard, 1984)," in Powrie, Babington, Davies, and Perriam, *Carmen on Film*, 122–131.

16 Françoise Pfaff, *A l'écoute du cinéma sénégalais* (Paris: L'Harmattan, 2010), 24–25.

17 Anjali Prabhu, "The 'Monumental' Heroine: Female Agency in Joseph Gaï Ramaka's *Karmen Gaï*," *Cinema Journal* 51, no. 4 (summer 2012): 86.

18 Lindiwe Dovey, *African Film and Literature: Adapting Violence to the Screen* (New York: Columbia University Press, 2009), 251.

19 Michael T. Martin, "I Am Not a Filmmaker Engagé: I Am An Ordinary Citizen Engagé," *Research in African Languages* 40 (2009): 210–211.

20 All references in this section are to material included with the DVD recording of *U-Carmen eKhayelitsha*, directed by Mark Ornford-May (Dimpho Di Kopane, 2005).

CONCLUSION

1 Adrian Rifkin, "Carmenology," *New Formations* 5 (summer 1988): 91.

2 Linda Hutcheon and Siobhan O'Flynn, *A Theory of Adaptation*, 2nd ed. (London and New York: Routledge, 2013), xx.

3 Niklas Luhmann, *Love as Passion: The Codification of Intimacy*, trans. Jeremy Gaines and Doris L. Jones (Cambridge, MA: Harvard University Press, 1986), 145.

4 Luhmann, *Love as Passion*, 45.

5 Jean Starobinski, *Enchantment: The Seductress in Opera*, trans. C. Jon Delogu (New York: Columbia University Press, 2008), 2.

6 Jean Baudrillard, *De la séduction* (Paris: Editions Galilée, 1979), 9–10.

7 *De vous, car nous l'avouons humblement, Et fort respectueusement, Quand il s'agit de tromperie, de duperie, de volerie, Il est toujour bon, sur ma foi, D'avoir les femmes avec soi, Et sans elles, Mes toutes belles, On ne fait jamais rien de bien* (Act II, Scene 2).

8 Adam Phillips, *On Flirtation* (Cambridge, MA: Harvard University Press, 1994), xviii.

9 Phillips, *On Flirtation*, xii.

10 Barthes, Fragments d'un discours amoureux, 39.

11 James Joyce, *Ulysses* (New York: Vintage, 1990), 333.

12 Luhmann, *Love as Passion*, 160.

13 Emmanuel Lévinas, *Le temps et l'autre* (Paris: Quadrige/Presses Universitaires de France, 1979), 63.

14 Barthes, *Roland Barthes par Roland Barthes*, 141.

For the benefit of digital users, indexed terms that span two pages (e.g., 52–53) may, on occasion, appear on only one of those pages.

Figures are indicated by *f* following the page number

on knowledge, 56–57
language in (*see under* language)
republished with other works, 54
on responsibility, 53, 65–67
Roma in (*see under* Roma/Gypsies)
science in, 54–55, 56–57,
    67–68, 72–73
sound as evidence of identification
    in, 53, 72
substitution of narrative
    voices in, 67
third chapter as source of Bizet's
    opera, 51–52
as unusual for operatic
    adaptation, 8–9
wit and ingenuity in, 53, 64
Carmen Disruption (Stephens), 113–14
Carmen Jones (film), 12, 82–83,
    83*f*, 102–3
Carmen on Film: A Cultural History
    (The Carmen Project), 75–76
Carmen on Ice (film), 119n4
Carmen Project, 75–76, 84–85
Carmen Suite (ballet), 119n3
Caruth, Cathy, 45–46
Cervantes, Miguel de, 3–4
Chaplin, Charlie, 2, 75–77, 76*f*, 92–93
Charnon-Deutsch, Lou, 72–73
Cixous, Hélène, 24
Clément, Catherine, 19, 23–24
Communards, 43–45
communism, 20
copyright lapse, 84
corrida trope, 85, 86–88
Corsaro, Frank, 20
culture, 1–2, 3–4, 5, 16, 33–34, 37–39,
    43, 47, 69, 73, 82–83, 88, 91, 92, 95,
    106–7, 112, 114–15

Dahlhaus, Carl, 47
Dame aux camélias, La (Dumas), 8–9
Dandridge, Dorothy, 82–83

Davies, Ann, 84
Dean, Winton, 36–37
Dear White People (film), 113–14
del Rio, Dolores, 77–79
del Sol, Laura, 91
Demeters, Maruschka, 92–93
DeMille, Cecil B., 75–77, 77*f*
dependency theme, 10–11, 12, 16, 19,
    20–21, 48–49
Desserre, Tommy, 119n3
Dimpho Di Kopane theater company,
    95, 100*f*, 100–3
Diouf, Abdou, 99–100
Djamileh (Bizet), 41–42, 43
Doane, Mary Ann, 28
Dom Juan (Molière), 37–38
Domingo, Plácido, 85
Don Giovanni (Mozart), 3–4, 37
Don Juan (character), 37–38
Dornford-May, Mark, 101
Doss, Thierno Ndiaye, 98–99
Dovey, Lindiwe, 99
Dumas, Alexandre, 8–9

Echo figure, 23–24, 36, 111
Equal Rights Amendment
    (proposed), 84–85
Escamillo (character), 20–26, 32–33, 37,
    79–80, 85–87, 101–2, 113–14
Esham, Faith, 85
Essay on the Inequality of the Races
    (Gobineau), 60
"European Obsession"
    (Charnon-Deutsch), 72–73
European Union, 91
evolution, 59
extra-diegetic commentary,
    96–97, 102–3

Falla, Manuel de, 89–91
Farrar, Geraldine, 76–77, 77*f*
fascism, 20

spectators, 39, 48–49
spoonerisms, 123n3
Starobinkski, Jean, 109–10
Stephens, Simon, 113–14
stock characters, 21–22
Stravinsky, Igor, 3–4
Stricker, Rémy, 45, 48
suffragette movement, 77–79
Suzuki, Seijun, 75–76

Tambling, Jeremy, 88
Tarot cards, 33–34, 66–67, 74, 100
Tchaikovsky, Modeste, 1–2
Tcherniakov, Dimitri, 113–14
Thatcher, Margaret, 84–85
Thomas, Debi, 119n4
Tirso de Molina, 3–4, 37–38
Townsend, Robert, 95–97, 96*f*, 102–3
Tragédie de Carmen, La (stage
    production), 64*f*
transcendence, 40
transgender Carmen, 113–14
Traviata, La (Verdi), 8–9
Turandot (Puccini), 48

U-Carmen (film), 12, 95, 100–2
Ulysses (Joyce), 111

une contre-pettrie, 123n3
University of Newcastle, 75–76, 77–79

Venice Film Festival, 92
Verdi, Giuseppe, 8–9
victim/victimizer roles, 16–19, 109, 110–11
Vidor, Charles, 80
Vitet (friend of Mérimée), 64

Wade, Abdoulaye, 99–100
Wagner, Richard, 15, 16, 38–39
Walsh, Raoul, 77–79
Winter Olympics of 1988, 2
Witt, Katarina, 119n4
women (roles and conditions of), 8,
    77–81, 84–85, 95, 101–2. *See also*
    feminism; gender; misogyny
World War I, 76–79

Xhosa, 100–1

Zakharova, Svetlana, 119n3
zeugma, 34, 36
Zigeuner, Die (Grellmann), 57–58
Zincali: Gypsies of Spain (Borrow), 57–58
Zuniga (character), 26–27, 32–33, 74,
    95–96